TWENTY-FIRST CENTURY
SMALL ARMS
THE WORLD'S GREAT INFANTRY WEAPONS

TWENTY-FIRST CENTURY
SMALL ARMS

THE WORLD'S GREAT INFANTRY WEAPONS

Steve Crawford

MBI

This edition first published in 2003 by MBI, an imprint of
MBI Publishing Company, Galtier Plaza, Suite 200, 380 Jackson Street,
St. Paul,
MN 55101-3885, USA

MBI titles are also available at discounts in bulk quantity for industrial
or sales-promotional use. For details write to Special Sales Manager at
Motorbooks International Wholesalers & Distributors, Galtier Plaza,
Suite 200, 380 Jackson Street, St. Paul, MN 55101-3885 USA.

ISBN: 0-7603-1503-5

Printed in China

Senior Editor: Peter Darman
Editor: Stephen Crane
Picture Research: Susannah Jayes
Design: Seth Grimbly
Production: Alastair Gourlay

PICTURE CREDITS
API: 28, 58, 63, 65, 67
Barrett Firearms: 91, 92, 93
FN Herstal: 12, 14, 16, 17, 18, 19, 20
Heckler & Koch: 29, 30, 31, 32, 33, 34, 35, 36, 37, 38, 39, 40, 41,
42, 43, 44, 45, 46
MPL: 27, 55, 89
Private collection: 8, 10, 54, 56, 59, 60, 61, 62, 68, 71, 77, 78, 82,
88, 94
Sako Ltd: 22, 23, 24
SIG: 79, 80, 81
Singapore Technologies Kinetics: 72, 73, 74
Steyr-Mannlicher AG: 6, 7, 9, 11
Tim Ripley: 47
TRH Pictures: 13, 15, 21, 25, 48, 49, 50, 51, 52, 53, 57, 64, 66, 69,
70, 95
US Department of Defense: 26, 75, 76, 83, 84, 85, 86, 90
Use by permission from Remington Arms Company, Inc.: 87

CONTENTS

CONTENTS

AUG-A1

The AUG (*Armee Universal Gewehr* – Universal Army Rifle) was developed by the Austrian company Steyr-Mannlicher AG in the 1970s and its production began in 1978. It was almost immediately adopted by the Austrian Army as the Stg 77 (*Sturmgewehr 77* – Assault Rifle, Model 1977). It later entered service with the armies of Australia, New Zealand, Oman, Malaysia, Saudi Arabia and Ireland, as well as with the US Coast Guard.

From the start the AUG was designed with versatility in mind: quick-interchange barrels (they can be removed and re-installed within seconds, even when hot, as a front grip is used as a barrel-replacement handle) of different lengths, and an ambidextrous fire capability. The AUG features an aluminium alloy receiver and polymer stock, bullpup layout, and conventional gas-powered action with rotating bolt. The bolt carrier itself rides on two guide rods and thus does not come into contact with the receiver. The left rod interoperates with the charging handle, while the right rod also acts as a gas piston. The hammer group is located in the butt-stock and is made almost entirely from polymer, including the hammer itself. The translucent magazine allows the user to see how much ammunition has been expended in action. Despite its looks the AUG is very strong, and in tests has worked after having been driven over by an army truck.

SPECIFICATIONS

Manufacturer:	*Steyr-Mannlicher AG*
Type:	*assault rifle*
Calibre:	*5.56mm*
Cartridge:	*5.56mm x 45mm M193 or NATO*
Length:	*790mm (31.1in)*
Length of barrel:	*508mm (20in)*
Number of grooves:	*6*
Weight:	*3.6kg (7.92lb)*
Cyclic rate of fire:	*650rpm*
Practical rate of fire:	*150rpm*
Operation:	*gas*
Magazine capacity:	*30*
Fire mode:	*semi-, full-auto*
Muzzle velocity:	*970mps (3182lps)*
Maximum range:	*1000m (3280ft)*
Effective range:	*400m (1312ft)*
Entered service:	*1978*

AUG-A2

The Steyr AUG-A2 is an improved version of the standard AUG assault rifle. It is a gas-operated, semi- and full-automatic assault rifle with a locked bolt action, quick-change barrel and integrated optical sight. The main difference between the A1 and A2 is the housing group: the A2 housing has a removable standard optical sight, which allows quick attachment of the Military Standard 1913 rail.

The A2 can be equipped with either a 407mm (16in) or 508mm (20in) barrel, each one having a gas regulator and a swing/pivot-type barrel grip. This gun's gas regulator has two action settings for firing, in order to ensure proper function under all environmental conditions. The "pull-through" trigger system fires semi-automatic when pulled halfway to a clearly felt point, and fires full-automatic when pulled fully back.

The bolt is of the fixed locking-turn variety, with eight locking lugs. The rifle can easily be changed from right to left-hand ejection by flipping the ejection port lid to the other side and installing a left-hand bolt (no tools are needed for this procedure). The AUG's modular concept allows for field stripping into the main groups within a few seconds. The casing can be olive drab, sand or black depending on user requirements.

SPECIFICATIONS

Manufacturer:	Steyr-Mannlicher AG
Type:	assault rifle
Calibre:	5.56mm
Cartridge:	5.56mm x 45mm M193 or NATO
Length:	690–790mm (27.16–31.1in)
Length of barrel:	407–508mm (16–20in)
Number of grooves:	6
Weight:	3.6kg (7.92lb)
Cyclic rate of fire:	650rpm
Practical rate of fire:	150rpm
Operation:	gas
Magazine capacity:	30
Fire mode:	semi-, full-auto
Muzzle velocity:	970mps (3182lps)
Maximum range:	1000m (3280ft)
Effective range:	400m (1312ft)
Entered service:	1981

AUG HBAR

The AUG assault rifle lends itself to a number of variants, including the HBAR (Heavy Barrelled Automatic Rifle), which has a 621mm (24in) barrel to become a light machine gun. With the strong Steyr bipod, the HBAR can also function as a sniping weapon. Well-designed, sturdy and mounted close to the muzzle, the bipod's legs elevate and lock like the venerable Mk I Bren bipod of World War II. When this barrel is used in the mode of a light support weapon, an open-bolt firing kit can be fitted to avoid "cook-offs" during sustained fire. Two large ports on each side and three small holes in front effectively control muzzle climb.

One thing that the HBAR lacks is a bayonet. There is a reason for this: the Austrian Army believes bayonets are archaic and inhumane, thus Austrian barrels don't have studs for bayonets. However, multi-purpose and lightweight bayonets are available to other users (a stud clamps on to mount them) should they request them.

The furniture is made from all high-impact plastic, which comes in military green, black and desert tan (the latter for Saudi use). Because the HBAR is a light support weapon, a 42-round magazine can be fitted in addition to the standard 30-round model. The longer barrel gives the HBAR a longer range, though weight increase is minimal.

SPECIFICATIONS

Manufacturer:	Steyr-Mannlicher AG
Type:	light support weapon
Calibre:	5.56mm
Cartridge:	5.56mm x 45mm M193 or NATO
Length:	900mm (35.43in)
Length of barrel:	621mm (24.45in)
Number of grooves:	6
Weight:	4.9kg (10.78lb)
Cyclic rate of fire:	680rpm
Practical rate of fire:	150rpm
Operation:	gas
Magazine capacity:	30 or 42 rounds
Fire mode:	semi-, full-auto
Muzzle velocity:	1000mps (320fps)
Maximum range:	1500m (4921ft)
Effective range:	500m (1640ft)
Entered service:	1980

AUG PARA

Taking advantage of the AUG's modularity, Steyr engineers have designed a kit which allows the user to convert an AUG into a 9mm carbine without the use of tools. The kit consists of a barrel group, bolt group, 25- or 32-round magazine and magazine adaptor. The carrier assembly differs from the .223 version in that it does not require the use of a rotating bolt. Also, the bolt allows only for right-handed ejection, so the stock's port cover must be situated accordingly on the left side. The magazine adaptor emulates the top of a .223 magazine and remains fixed to the stock during magazine changes. It contains its own bolt hold-open actuator, which is triggered by the 9mm magazine follower. Because it utilizes the blowback principle, there is no gas port or piston in the 406mm (16in) barrel assembly. A 9mm AUG measures 665mm (26in) in length and is marginally shorter than a Heckler & Koch MP5A2 submachine gun, which uses a 225mm (8.85in) barrel.

As the AUG is a system, four different barrels fit any receiver in a matter of seconds. This makes four different weapons. All barrels are constructed of high-quality steel by the cold-hammer forging process developed by GFM of Steyr, Austria, and bores and chambers are chrome-plated to increase barrel life. Barrels have six grooves with a right-hand twist of one turn in 229mm (9in).

SPECIFICATIONS

Manufacturer:	Steyr-Mannlicher AG
Type:	assault rifle
Calibre:	9mm
Cartridge:	9mm Parabellum
Length:	665mm (26in)
Length of barrel:	406mm (16in)
Number of grooves:	6
Weight:	3.3kg (7.26lb)
Cyclic rate of fire:	700rpm
Practical rate of fire:	150rpm
Operation:	blowback
Magazine capacity:	25 or 32
Fire mode:	semi-, full-auto
Muzzle velocity:	400mps (1312fps)
Maximum range:	400m (1312ft)
Effective range:	50m (164ft)
Entered service:	1986

MPi 69

This submachine gun has a receiver made from bent and welded sheet steel that is carried in the frame unit. The magazine feeds in through the pistol grip, and the bolt is of the "wrap-around" or "telescoped" type: the actual bolt face is well back within the bolt and much of the bolt mass is in front of the breech at the moment of firing. This system allows the maximum mass for the minimum bolt stroke and assists in producing a compact weapon. Cocking is performed by pulling on the carry sling, which is attached at the forward end to the cocking knob (a bracket welded into the top of the receiver ensures that the cocking action can only be performed when the sling is held at right angles to the receiver, on the left-hand side). The normal pull from the top of the weapon, as when slinging it over the shoulder, cannot move the cocking piece.

There is a safety catch in the form of a cross-bolt above the trigger which locks the trigger when set to safe. It is a three-position bolt; when pushed across to the right so that a white "S" protrudes, it is safe; when pushed across to the left so that a red "F" protrudes, it is set for automatic fire. There is also a halfway position in which single shots are possible.

Overall the MPi 69 is easy to strip and re-assemble, and is a well-designed and robust submachine gun.

SPECIFICATIONS

Manufacturer:	Steyr-Mannlicher AG
Type:	submachine gun
Calibre:	9mm
Cartridge:	9mm Parabellum
Length:	465–670mm (18.31–26.38in)
Length of barrel:	260mm (10.24in)
Number of grooves:	6
Weight:	3.13kg (6.88lb)
Cyclic rate of fire:	550rpm
Practical rate of fire:	200rpm
Operation:	blowback
Magazine capacity:	25 or 32
Fire mode:	semi-, full-auto
Muzzle velocity:	381mps (1250fps)
Maximum range:	100m (328ft)
Effective range:	50m (164ft)
Entered service:	1969

SSG PIV

The Steyr SSG 69 was adopted by the Austrian Army in 1969. It is a bolt-action, rotating bolt, magazine-fed rifle which is an excellent weapon and has been produced in a number of variants, including models with heavy barrels, short barrels and silencers. The barrel is cold-hammer forged and the standard feeding device is a detachable Steyr-type rotary magazine.

The Steyr SSG is offered to military, police and civilian shooters in four different models: the SSG PI, SSG PII, SSG PIIK and the SSG PIV. The SSG PI was originally developed as a counter-sniper rifle, and was the first such weapon to be equipped with a synthetic stock. It has a 660mm (26in) barrel and is equipped with iron sights, as well as standard NATO-specified dovetails for a telescopic sight. The SSG PII is built for police use as a tactical or sniper rifle. It has a heavy barrel, lacks iron sights and has an oversized bolt handle for quick follow-up shots (essential for hostage-rescue operations when multiple targets often present themselves). The SSG PIIK differs from the SSG PII only by a shorter barrel and is for use in crowded urban situations – despite the shorter barrel accuracy is not degraded up to a range of 500m (1640ft). The SSG PIV has a 406mm (16in) barrel with detachable flash hider, which can easily be changed to a sound suppressor (silencer).

SPECIFICATIONS

Manufacturer:	*Steyr-Mannlicher AG*
Type:	*sniper rifle*
Calibre:	*7.62mm*
Cartridge:	*7.62 x 51mm NATO*
Length:	*896mm (35.27in)*
Length of barrel:	*406mm (16in)*
Number of grooves:	*4*
Weight:	*3.9kg (8.58lb)*
Cyclic rate of fire:	*n/a*
Practical rate of fire:	*5rpm*
Operation:	*bolt*
Magazine capacity:	*5*
Fire mode:	*single shot*
Muzzle velocity:	*860mps (2822fps)*
Maximum range:	*2000m (6561ft)*
Effective range:	*1000m (3280ft)*
Entered service:	*1969*

F2000

The F2000 allows accessories to be added while respecting the ergonomics, balance and smooth lines of an assault rifle. Space is provided inside the weapon for a centralized power pack, and it can be used by left-handed firers without modifications thanks to the forward ejection. The bullpup design gives a very compact rifle with a full-length barrel. Light, with excellent balance, and with a smooth outer shape, the F2000 is easy and comfortable to carry. The firing selector and magazine catch are easily accessed.

For a grenade to be effective it must hit within a few metres of the target. In operational conditions this is very difficult. Grenades are heavy projectiles launched at low velocity, so they normally have a high, curved trajectory. Few grenades land close to their target, and initial volleys are almost always well off target.

The F2000's fire control system provides a means of quickly and accurately aiming the grenade launcher, which greatly increases its effect. It ensures a high probability of achieving an effective hit with a minimum number of grenades. A laser rangefinder first determines the range to the target and then a ballistic computer, programmed with three firing tables, automatically calculates the launch angle. An infra-red laser pointer allows aiming at night.

SPECIFICATIONS

Manufacturer:	FN Herstal
Type:	integrated weapon system
Calibre:	5.56mm
Cartridge:	5.56 x 45mm NATO
Length:	694mm (27.32in)
Length of barrel:	400mm (15.74in)
Number of grooves:	unknown
Weight:	3.6kg (7.92lb)
Cyclic rate of fire:	850rpm
Practical rate of fire:	unknown
Operation:	gas
Magazine capacity:	30
Fire mode:	unknown
Muzzle velocity:	900mps (2952fps)
Maximum range:	unknown
Effective range:	unknown
Entered service:	not yet in service

FN FAL

The FAL is a gas-operated rifle and fires from the closed-bolt position in both the semi- and full-auto modes. It has an operator-adjustable gas regulator which works on the "exhaust" principle. Under ideal conditions the major portion of the gas is passed through the regulator and out into the air, which helps to reduce recoil.

The trigger mechanism of the FAL is well designed and has been copied around the world. It incorporates both the usual sear, which is attached to the trigger by a pin, and an "automatic safety sear" which is in front of the hammer and must be depressed for the hammer to rotate.

Originally the FAL was designed to fire the 7.92mm round, but once NATO opted for the 7.62mm round the rifle was redesigned to accept this calibre. The FAL was an instant success and though not particularly compact or light, it is very accurate and robust. The FAL always fires from a closed bolt, and most models can fire both semi- or full-automatic. That said, the 7.62mm round is really too powerful for controllable, hand-held automatic fire. One valuable feature is the adjustable gas plug that controls the amount of gas diverted against the piston. If the rifle becomes fouled in dusty conditions, for example, the extra gas pressure will overcome any tendency to jam. The FAL is undoubtedly one of the greatest assault rifles ever built.

SPECIFICATIONS

Manufacturer:	*FN Herstal*
Type:	*assault rifle*
Calibre:	*7.62mm*
Cartridge:	*7.62 x 51mm NATO*
Length:	*1090mm (42.9in)*
Length of barrel:	*533mm (20.98in)*
Number of grooves:	*4*
Weight:	*4.25kg (9.35lb)*
Cyclic rate of fire:	*650–700rpm*
Practical rate of fire:	*200rpm*
Operation:	*gas*
Magazine capacity:	*20*
Fire mode:	*semi-, full-auto*
Muzzle velocity:	*840mps (2756fps)*
Maximum range:	*1200m (3937ft)*
Effective range:	*550m (1804ft)*
Entered service:	*1953*

FN FNC

The gas-operated FNC rifle was a replacement for FN's CAL rifle (which was a scaled-down version of the FAL, using the same gas system and tipping bolt) and fires from a closed bolt. Mounted above the barrel, the gas cylinder has six ports 38mm (1.5in) behind the barrel's gas vent. At the end of this short stroke, all gases escape the cylinder when the piston head passes the exhaust ports. A handle welded to the rear of the gas cylinder rotates the cylinder, opening and closing a small port in the gas block. When the adjustment handle is rotated to the left, this gas block port is exposed and a small amount of the propellant gases escapes before the piston begins its rearward travel.

The FNC can fire grenades from its muzzle with blank ammunition using a sheet-metal, flip-up, combination grenade sight/gas valve called the alidade. The alidade is attached to the gas block/front sight assembly. When pivoted up to the vertical position, the alidade axis turns to close the gas vent. Then all gases propel the grenade. Using this procedure all propellant gases bypass the gas system, thus the weapon does not cycle and the bolt must be retracted manually.

The FNC has a slab-sided receiver, and a round, ribbed fore-end with flutes. It is a selective-fire weapon which also has a three-round burst facility.

SPECIFICATIONS

Manufacturer:	*FN Herstal*
Type:	*assault rifle*
Calibre:	*5.56mm*
Cartridge:	*5.56 x 45mm NATO*
Length:	*756–1000mm (29.76in–39.37in)*
Length of barrel:	*449mm (17.68in)*
Number of grooves:	*6*
Weight:	*3.8kg (8.36lb)*
Cyclic rate of fire:	*650–700rpm*
Practical rate of fire:	*200rpm*
Operation:	*gas*
Magazine capacity:	*30*
Fire mode:	*semi-, full-auto, three-round burst*
Muzzle velocity:	*965mps (3166fps)*
Maximum range:	*600m (1968ft)*
Effective range:	*450m (1476ft)*
Entered service:	*1976*

FN MAG

The FN *Mitrailleuse d'Appui Général* (MAG), meaning General Purpose Machine Gun, has been adopted by more than 20 countries, including USA (under the designation M240), Great Britain (L7 GPMG), Israel, India and Sweden. All MAGs and its derivatives have quick-interchangeable barrels that can be swapped in a battlefield environment (an essential facility as machine-gun barrels overheat when subjected to intensive combat use). When mounted on a bipod the MAG is an infantry support weapon; on a heavier tripod it becomes a heavy support weapon. It can also be mounted on vehicle turrets or pintles for primary, coaxial or air-defence purposes.

The gas piston sits inside the cylinder and is connected to an extension piece and a piston post. A slot in the extension piece allows empty gases to pass through and be ejected beneath the gun. When the weapon is cocked the piston and piston port are pulled back against the return spring, pulling the bolt with them. Next they fly forward, and the bolt takes the next round from the ammunition belt. Normal sights are a leaf rear sight, which is folded upright for long ranges but laid down as a sight for short- and medium-range firing. The basic MAG has a wooden butt, smooth barrel, pistol grip and slotted flash eliminator. However, different armies have tailored the weapon to their own preferences.

SPECIFICATIONS

Manufacturer:	*FN Herstal*
Type:	*machine gun*
Calibre:	*7.62mm*
Cartridge:	*7.62 x 51mm NATO*
Length:	*1250mm (49.2in)*
Length of barrel:	*546mm (21.5in)*
Number of grooves:	*4*
Weight:	*10.15kg (22.33lb)*
Cyclic rate of fire:	*850rpm*
Practical rate of fire:	*200rpm*
Operation:	*gas*
Magazine capacity:	*metal link belt*
Fire mode:	*full-auto*
Muzzle velocity:	*853mps (2800fps)*
Maximum range:	*3000m (9842ft)*
Effective range:	*1800m (5905ft)*
Entered service:	*1955*

M240G

After extensive tests, the US Army selected the M240B 7.62mm medium machine gun produced by Fabrique Nationale as a replacement for the M60 machine gun. The M240 is a licence-produced version of the FN MAG. This is a ground-mounted variant of the original M240/M240C/M240E1 coaxial/pintle-mounted machine gun used on M2/M3 Bradley infantry fighting vehicles, the M1 Abrams main battle tank, and the US Marine Corps' Light Armored Vehicles (LAVs). While possessing many of the same basic characteristics as the M60 medium machine gun, the M240 has superior reliability and maintainability compared to the M60.

The M240D 7.62mm machine gun is a left-hand feed, gas-operated, air-cooled, fixed headspace weapon. It can be configured for two roles: aircraft and ground. In the aircraft configuration the M240D has a front and rear sight and a trigger group which accommodates the spade grip device.

The M240G version has a bipod and can also be mounted on a tripod if need be. Thus in this guise the weapon reverts back to its original ground role. There are some minor differences between the M240G and the FN MAG due to the lengthy development history, but essentially the US version has retained the reliability and robustness of its venerable Belgian parent.

SPECIFICATIONS

Manufacturer:	*FN Herstal*
Type:	*medium machine gun*
Calibre:	*7.62mm*
Cartridge:	*7.62 x 51mm NATO*
Length:	*1220mm (48.03in)*
Length of barrel:	*627mm (24.68in)*
Number of grooves:	*4*
Weight:	*11.7kg (25.74lb)*
Cyclic rate of fire:	*750rpm*
Practical rate of fire:	*200rpm*
Operation:	*gas*
Magazine capacity:	*metal link belt*
Fire mode:	*full-auto*
Muzzle velocity:	*854mps (2800fps)*
Maximum range:	*3725m (12,221ft)*
Effective range:	*1800m (5905ft)*
Entered service:	*1995*

M249

The M249 is essentially the FN Minimi Squad Automatic Weapon (SAW) with some variations to meet US military specifications. The main external differences are in the shape of the butt and fore-end/hand-guard. It has a regulator for selecting either normal (750 rounds per minute) or maximum (1000 rounds per minute) rate of fire. The M249 can be fired from the shoulder, hip or under-arm position. When employed as a machine gun it can be mounted on either a bipod or tripod, though barrels must not be interchanged with those from other M249s unless the headspace has been set for that weapon by direct support personnel.

The M249 is fed from a 200-round disintegrating belt, but is also capable of firing ammunition from standard M16 magazines inserted into a magazine well in the bottom of the SAW (a useful attribute for battlefield use when ammunition can often be in scarce supply). The M249 is used to engage dismounted infantry, crew-served weapons, anti-tank guided missile teams and thin-skinned vehicles. It has become the standard automatic rifle of the US Army infantry squad. The Belgian Minimi entered service in Europe in 1974, though the weapon entered service with the US armed forces in 1990. The specifications at right refer to the American variant of the weapon.

SPECIFICATIONS

Manufacturer:	FN Herstal
Type:	squad automatic weapon
Calibre:	5.56mm
Cartridge:	5.56 x 45mm NATO
Length:	1040mm (40.9in)
Length of barrel:	523mm (20.59in)
Number of grooves:	6
Weight:	6.85kg (15.07lb)
Cyclic rate of fire:	750–1000rpm
Practical rate of fire:	200rpm
Operation:	gas
Magazine capacity:	200-round metal link belt
Fire mode:	full-auto
Muzzle velocity:	915mps (300fps)
Maximum range:	3600m (11,811ft)
Effective range:	1000m (3280ft)
Entered service:	1990

MINIMI PARA

The Minimi Para is a compact version of the Minimi with a short barrel and a sliding butt. The Minimi's rotary gas regulator is a simplification of the FN MAG's regulator. It has two positions, normal and adverse, and is hand-adjustable. The adverse position increases the cyclic rate, though this means reliability will deteriorate due to the increased cyclic rate. The only real disadvantage to gas systems is an increase in fouling over recoil-operated weapons, a problem compounded by the current emphasis on the use of ball-type powders.

The Minimi has a chrome-lined bore and a three-second quick-change barrel, and its feed cover can be closed with the bolt in any position along the feed cam. The tubular-aluminium skeleton stock and its folding wire buttstrap are weight-saving contributions. The Minimi's push-button safety and elimination of the semi-automatic mode simplify the sear mechanism. A loaded belt indicator has been provided for night use, and the rear sight is adjustable to 1000m (3280ft). The Para version has been designed for airborne troops and is an extremely reliable weapon. The bolt is a two-piece model, with the bolt face locking into the barrel extension by means of locking lugs. A cam system on the bolt carrier causes the bolt to unlock, in a similar manner to that employed in assault rifles.

SPECIFICATIONS

Manufacturer:	FN Herstal
Type:	light machine gun
Calibre:	5.56mm
Cartridge:	5.56 x 45mm NATO
Length:	893mm (35.15in)
Length of barrel:	347mm (13.66in)
Number of grooves:	6
Weight:	7.1kg (15.62lb)
Cyclic rate of fire:	850rpm
Practical rate of fire:	200rpm
Operation:	gas
Magazine capacity:	30 or 200-round belt
Fire mode:	full-auto
Muzzle velocity:	900mps (2952fps)
Maximum range:	3600m (11,811ft)
Effective range:	1000m (3280ft)
Entered service:	1974

MINIMI SPW

The Special Purpose Weapon (SPW), which is shown above with the Para model (the SPW variant is the bottom weapon) is a special model of the M249 Minimi machine gun developed to meet a US Special Operations requirement for a lightweight variant of the M249 that would retain the intrinsic functionality and reliability of the standard model. The total reduction in weight is 1.86kg (4.1lb) – weight saving is always an imperative for special operations forces. In addition, a new lightweight barrel has been developed and the carrying handle, the magazine well and the mount lugs (for vehicle applications) have been removed. Unique to the M249 SPW are special rails to accommodate scopes, laser designators and flashlights; plus a pistol grip and a detachable bipod.

The SPW features a quick-change barrel with a fixed headspace, and an integral sight rail for an optical sight. In addition, there is a multi-rail forearm for use with additional accessories. As with the standard Minimi, the SPW version is a very reliable weapon. The SPW can also fire from M16 magazines if necessary, and when firing from a magazine the cyclic rate of fire is much faster than from a belt as the mechanism does not need to lift the weight of the 200-round belt. That said, magazine feed is really only a secondary option to be used in an emergency.

SPECIFICATIONS

Manufacturer:	*FN Herstal*
Type:	*special forces machine gun*
Calibre:	*5.56mm*
Cartridge:	*5.56 x 45mm NATO*
Length:	*775–908mm (30.5–35.75in)*
Length of barrel:	*406mm (16in)*
Number of grooves:	*6*
Weight:	*8.77kg (19.3lb)*
Cyclic rate of fire:	*850rpm*
Practical rate of fire:	*200rpm*
Operation:	*gas*
Magazine capacity:	*100- or 200-round belt*
Fire mode:	*full-auto*
Muzzle velocity:	*915mps (3000fps)*
Maximum range:	*3600m (11,811ft)*
Effective range:	*450m (1476ft)*
Entered service:	*unknown*

P90

The P90 was developed as a lightweight, small submachine gun with a large magazine capacity and low recoil. Capable of easily penetrating body armour, the P90 has been adopted by numerous government agencies all over the world.

The P90 looks very unconventional, with its top-loaded magazine, polymer construction, integral sights and an unusual stock. The weapon uses a simple blowback mechanism, and the entire barrel/bolt assembly can be lifted out of the weapon in seconds. Attached directly to this assembly is the sight, which is a non-enlarging scope and features a recticle which is highly visible in all but the very poorest of light conditions. For emergency use there are also normal sights on either side of the scope (the P90 is also fully ambidextrous).

The likelihood of dirt fouling the mechanism is minimal because when the magazine is loaded there are only two ways that dirt can enter the weapon: through the barrel or the ejection port. However, the latter is located on the underside of the weapon, which makes it unlikely that much dirt will enter via this route. Because of this, cartridges are ejected downwards (a case catcher which can hold 100 empty cases and snaps onto the ejection port is available). Other available extras are lasers, lamps and silencers.

SPECIFICATIONS

Manufacturer:	*FN Herstal*
Type:	*personal defence weapon*
Calibre:	*5.7mm*
Cartridge:	*5.7 x 28mm*
Length:	*500mm (19.68in)*
Length of barrel:	*263mm (10.35in)*
Number of grooves:	*8*
Weight:	*2.54kg (5.58lb)*
Cyclic rate of fire:	*900rpm*
Practical rate of fire:	*200rpm*
Operation:	*blowback*
Magazine capacity:	*50*
Fire mode:	*semi-, full-auto*
Muzzle velocity:	*715mps (2345fps)*
Maximum range:	*400m (1312ft)*
Effective range:	*200m (656ft)*
Entered service:	*1990*

TYPE 56

This is one of the many Kalashnikov clones that have been manufactured around the world, though like most Chinese copies it is inferior to the original with regard to quality of parts and engineering.

The Type 56 assault rifle was adopted by the People's Liberation Army in 1956, along with the Type 56 carbine (which is a licence-built Soviet SKS copy). The Type 56 assault rifle is, in turn, also a licensed copy of the Soviet AK-47 assault rifle, with minor modifications. The Type 56 is a gas-operated, selective-fire weapon, i.e. it fires both semi-automatic and full-automatic. The receiver is machined from steel, and the two-lugged bolt locks into the receiver walls. It has AK-47-style controls with reciprocating charging handle and massive safety/fire selector lever on the right side of the receiver. The furniture is made from wood, and the compact version with an underfolding metallic buttstock was also produced. The only visible difference between the Type 56 and the AK-47 is a permanently attached spike bayonet, which folds under the barrel when not in use. The Type 56-2 variant has a skeleton, tubular-type buttstock which folds to the right side of the receiver. The Type 56-C model appears to be a copy of the Russian AK-74 assault rifle, with plastic furniture. The side-folding butt has a cheek-piece and new muzzle compensator.

SPECIFICATIONS

Manufacturer:	*State Factories*
Type:	*assault rifle*
Calibre:	*7.62mm*
Cartridge:	*7.62 x 39mm M1943*
Length:	*869mm (34.21ft)*
Length of barrel:	*414mm (16.3in)*
Number of grooves:	*4*
Weight:	*4.3kg (9.46lb)*
Cyclic rate of fire:	*775rpm*
Practical rate of fire:	*400rpm*
Operation:	*gas*
Magazine capacity:	*30*
Fire mode:	*semi-, full-auto*
Muzzle velocity:	*710mps (2329fps)*
Maximum range:	*1000m (3280ft)*
Effective range:	*400m (1312ft)*
Entered service:	*1956*

TRG-22

The TRG range of sniper rifles was developed by the Finnish company Sako. The original models, the TRG-21 and TRG-41, were both built around Sako's TRG bolt action, with a rotating bolt having three massive lugs at the front. The same action is also used in Sako's TRG-S rifle. Other key features of the TRG sniper rifles are aluminium bedded, composite stocks with adjustable butts and cheek-pieces, heavy, match-grade barrels (which are cold-hammered with muzzle brakes) and adjustable triggers. The main difference between the TRG-21 and TRG-41 is in the ammunition used. The TRG-21 is designed to fire standard 7.62mm NATO ammunition, while the TRG-41 is designed to fire the more powerful .338 Lapua Magnum cartridge, and has a large (magnum-size) action and a longer barrel with muzzle brake. In all other respects both rifles are similar.

The TRG-22 and TRG-42 are upgraded versions of the TRG-21 and TRG-41 rifles respectively, with modified stocks and some internal changes. New stocks have slightly different contours and there are integral folding bipods at the front. Sako sniper rifles are renowned for their accuracy and strength. As a result, they are used by many European police and counter-terrorist units. They are among the élite of Europe's sniper rifles.

SPECIFICATIONS

Manufacturer:	Sako Ltd
Type:	sniper rifle
Calibre:	.308in
Cartridge:	.308 Winchester
Length:	1150mm (45.24in)
Length of barrel:	660mm (26in)
Number of grooves:	4
Weight:	4.7kg (10.25lb)
Cyclic rate of fire:	n/a
Practical rate of fire:	10rpm
Operation:	bolt
Magazine capacity:	10
Fire mode:	single shot
Muzzle velocity:	914mps (2998fps)
Maximum range:	2000m (6561ft)
Effective range:	800m (2624ft)
Entered service:	1991

TRG-42

The TRG range of sniper rifles have receivers made using the cold-hammering method, and they are stabilized with three fastening screws. The magazine is a detachable, centre-fed model which holds five rounds. The double-stage trigger pull is adjustable from 1 to 2.5kg (2 to 5lb), and is also adjustable in length and horizontal or vertical pitch. The entire trigger assembly, including the trigger guard, can be removed from the rifle without disassembling any other part of the rifle.

The safety catch, which is silent in operation, is positioned inside the trigger guard. The safety locks the trigger mechanism and locks the bolt in a closed position with the firing pin blocked. The base of the stock is made of aluminium, to which the polyurethane forestock is attached. The buttstock is also made of polyurethane and is reinforced through the use of an aluminium skeleton. Spacers allow the cheekpiece to be fully adjustable in height and infinitely adjustable in windage and pitch. As with many modern rifles, the stock is designed for both right- and left-handed shooters. The buttplate is adjustable both for distance and angle through the use of spacers, and is also infinitely adjustable in height and pitch.

Though the TRG is supplied with open sights, there is an integral dovetail on the top of the receiver for other sights.

SPECIFICATIONS

Manufacturer:	Sako Ltd
Type:	sniper rifle
Calibre:	.338in
Cartridge:	.338 Lapua Magnum
Length:	1200mm (47.24in)
Length of barrel:	690mm (27.16in)
Number of grooves:	4
Weight:	5.1kg (11.22lb)
Cyclic rate of fire:	n/a
Practical rate of fire:	10rpm
Operation:	bolt
Magazine capacity:	5
Fire mode:	single shot
Muzzle velocity:	914mps (2998fps)
Maximum range:	2000m (6561ft)
Effective range:	800m (2624ft)
Entered service:	1991

TRG-S

The TRG-S is based on a bolt-action hunting rifle with a detachable clip magazine. The single-stage trigger pull is adjustable from 1 to 2kg (2.2 to 4.4lb), and the design of the stock and pistol grip makes the rifle suitable for both right- and left-handed shooters. The straightline stock reduces recoil, which means the rifle is controllable even under arduous tactical circumstances. The stock length and heelplate angle can be easily adjusted with straight or angle spacers. The above photograph shows the TRG-S equipped with open sights with post bead, but the company also supplies this model without open sights. There are integral rails for scope mounts on top of the receiver.

The free-floating barrel is cold-hammer forged, and the company can supply stainless steel barrels if required. In addition, an optional detachable muzzle brake can be fitted, which acts as an efficient flash-hider. The TRG-S is an excellent weapon, though its three-round magazine could be considered a handicap in some tactical situations.

Sako also produce a number of accessories for their sniper rifle range. These include a suppressor (for .308in Winchester calibre), a foldable bipod, auxiliary steel peep sights for emergency use, a match sight mounting set, a night set adaptor, plus different slings, swivels, cleaning sets and transit cases.

SPECIFICATIONS

Manufacturer:	*Sako Ltd*
Type:	*sniper rifle*
Calibre:	*.338in*
Cartridge:	*.338 Lapua Magnum*
Length:	*1200mm (47.24in)*
Length of barrel:	*660mm (26in)*
Number of grooves:	*4*
Weight:	*3.7kg (8.14lb)*
Cyclic rate of fire:	*n/a*
Practical rate of fire:	*5rpm*
Operation:	*bolt*
Magazine capacity:	*3*
Fire mode:	*single shot*
Muzzle velocity:	*914mps (2998fps)*
Maximum range:	*2000m (6561ft)*
Effective range:	*800m (2624ft)*
Entered service:	*1995*

AA 52

The French AA 52 machine gun is more correctly termed the *Arme Automatique Transformable Modèle 1952*. It was the first machine gun to be designed and produced in France after World War II as a general purpose lightweight weapon. A later version was produced to take the NATO standard 7.62mm round, and was called the AA 7.62 F-1. This weapon has the same dimensions, but has a muzzle velocity of 830mps (2723fps) with a light barrel and 845mps (2772fps) with a heavy barrel.

The AA 52 is a belt-fed 7.5mm machine gun. A fairly mundane weapon, it is still used in the French Foreign Legion today. Because of the inaccuracy of the weapon, it can pepper-spread a large area to the front – a useful application in certain military scenarios. The weapon is simple and sturdy in construction, and stripping and assembly is not a problem. It is supplied with a bipod and sling for carrying. It has a hump-backed receiver and is belt-fed from the left. When mounted on a tripod a heavier barrel is used. The AA 52 is air-cooled and employs a two-piece bolt and fluted chamber. The heavy barrelled version can be mounted on a US M2 tripod for the sustained-fire role. With a heavier barrel the range is increased.

The specifications at right refer to the heavy barrelled version of the weapon.

SPECIFICATIONS

Manufacturer:	MAS
Type:	general purpose machine gun
Calibre:	7.5mm
Cartridge:	7.5 x 54mm French M1929
Length:	1080–1245mm (42.5–49in)
Length of barrel:	600mm (23.62in)
Number of grooves:	4
Weight:	11.37kg (25.01lb)
Cyclic rate of fire:	700rpm
Practical rate of fire:	100rpm
Operation:	delayed blowback
Magazine capacity:	disintegrating link belt
Fire mode:	full-automatic
Muzzle velocity:	823mps (2700fps)
Maximum range:	1800m (5905ft)
Effective range:	1000m (3280ft)
Entered service:	1952

FAMAS

The FAMAS was developed in the 1970s and entered service with the French Army in the early 1980s. The barrel is only fractionally shorter than that of the American M16 assault rifle, but the entire rifle is some 250mm (9.84in) shorter overall thanks to its bullpup design. It operates by a delayed blowback system based on a two-part bolt. When the trigger is pulled the case sets back against the light bolt head, and this force is transmitted to a lever which is engaged with a recess in the receiver. As the lever is turned, it has to force the heavy bolt body back at a mechanical disadvantage, so slowing the opening of the bolt.

There is the usual semi-automatic or full-automatic option, and in addition the rifle can be set to fire a three-round burst. There is a bipod for steadier shooting and a sling is also provided for off-hand firing and for use when launching grenades. The iron sights are concealed inside the channel section of the long carrying handle, beneath which is the cocking handle.

Nicknamed *Le Clairon* (The Bugle) by French troops, the FAMAS is an effective and accurate weapon. The F1 is the French military version. The G2 is the updated, NATO-standardized version and is in use outside France. Its magazine housing can accept any M16-type magazine, and the safety/selector is inside the trigger guard.

SPECIFICATIONS

Manufacturer:	MAS
Type:	assault rifle
Calibre:	5.56mm
Cartridge:	5.56 x 45mm French
Length:	757mm (29.8in)
Length of barrel:	508mm (20in)
Number of grooves:	4
Weight:	3.7kg (8.14lb)
Cyclic rate of fire:	950rpm
Practical rate of fire:	200rpm
Operation:	delayed blowback
Magazine capacity:	30
Fire mode:	semi-, full-auto, three-round burst
Muzzle velocity:	960mps (3150fps)
Maximum range:	1000m (3280ft)
Effective range:	400m (1312ft)
Entered service:	1980

FR-F2

The FR-F1 bolt-action sniper rifle was developed from the old Model 36 rifle (which was a bolt-action repeater, with the bolt locking into the receiver behind the magazine), and had a padded cheek rest and an adjustable buttstock, using a spacer system. The FR-F2 is an updated version of the FR-F1, which uses a different bipod/stock configuration and has some other general upgrades, such as a fore-end made of plastic-covered metal. The bipod is attached to a yoke around the barrel, and the barrel itself is covered with a thermal sleeve to reduce heat haze in the sight line. In addition, the bipod has been shifted rearwards to the front edge of the receiver. The bolt handle slopes forward, as with the F1. Both weapons have been around for quite some time, and while they are not at the cutting end of technology they have proven themselves reliable weapons. The FR-F2 is currently the standard-issue sniper rifle for the French military. Like Great Britain, France has opted to keep faith with bolt-action sniper rifles on the battlefield.

Iron sights are fitted as standard, but to use them the telescopic scope must be removed. Once the scope is zeroed it can be removed and replaced without further modification. The F1 model was originally in 7.5mm calibre, but later models were produced in 7.62mm chambering.

SPECIFICATIONS

Manufacturer:	MAS
Type:	sniper rifle
Calibre:	7.62mm
Cartridge:	7.62 x 51mm NATO
Length:	1138mm (44.8in)
Length of barrel:	552mm (21.73in)
Number of grooves:	4
Weight:	5.2kg (11.44lb)
Cyclic rate of fire:	n/a
Practical rate of fire:	10rpm
Operation:	bolt
Magazine capacity:	10
Fire mode:	single shot
Muzzle velocity:	852mps (2795fps)
Maximum range:	2000m (6561ft)
Effective range:	800m (2624ft)
Entered service:	1984

G3

I n 1950, the Spanish Army issued a requirement for a modern selective-fire rifle. Development began at the *Centro de Estudios Tecnicos de Materiales Especiales*, an agency of the Spanish Government known as CETME. CETME assembled a team of Spanish and German weapon designers. The team included Ludwig Vorgrimmler, generally recognized as the inventor of the delayed roller-locking system. The breech mechanism of the StG.45 (M) was used as the basis for the new design. Prototypes of the new rifle were available for firing by 1952. By 1954, the 7.62mm x 51 cartridge had been standardized by the NATO alliance. The Spanish Government approached Heckler & Koch for adaptation of the CETME rifle in this new calibre in 1954. After another five years of development, the West German Army adopted the new rifle in 1959, and gave it its new name, G3 (*Gewehr* 3).

All G3s suffer from heaviness and excessive recoil of the 7.62 x 51 cartridge in the automatic-fire mode. That said, the stopping power of the 7.62mm round is much better than the 5.56m bullet, and has greater range. Like all Heckler & Koch weapons, the G3 is very reliable and very robust. There was extensive use of steel pressings in this selective-fire weapon. It has undergone extensive modifications since it entered service in 1959.

SPECIFICATIONS

Manufacturer:	*Heckler & Koch*
Type:	*assault rifle*
Calibre:	*7.62mm*
Cartridge:	*7.62 x 51mm NATO*
Length:	*1021mm (40.2in)*
Length of barrel:	*450mm (17.72in)*
Number of grooves:	*4*
Weight:	*4.4kg (9.68lb)*
Cyclic rate of fire:	*550rpm*
Practical rate of fire:	*150rpm*
Operation:	*delayed blowback*
Magazine capacity:	*20*
Fire mode:	*semi-, full-auto*
Muzzle velocity:	*800mps (2625fps)*
Maximum range:	*1500m (4921ft)*
Effective range:	*550m (1804ft)*
Entered service:	*1959*

G36

The new G36/G36E is a true modular weapon system in 5.56 x 45mm calibre, which was designed for the German Army as a replacement for the G11 assault rifle. Constructed almost entirely of a tough, fibre-reinforced polymer material and using a simple, self-regulating gas system, the G36/G36E provides the user with a lightweight weapon that delivers high performance with extremely low maintenance.

The barrel of the G36/G36E can be exchanged by unit armourers to create either a rifle or a carbine, using the same common receiver. The G36 can fire frangible training ammunition without special muzzle devices. Blank and safety blank-firing devices that use conventional blank ammunition are also available as accessories.

The G36 gas system is insensitive to fouling back into the weapon's interior. This ensures reliable operation even after firing more than 15,000 rounds without cleaning. Polymer components can easily be cleaned with water-based cleaning solutions, or even water if necessary. The 30-round translucent polymer magazines can lock together without a magazine clamp, are 30 percent lighter than metal magazines and are corrosion proof. The ambidextrous cocking lever doubles as a forward assist and can be used to chamber a round silently.

SPECIFICATIONS

Manufacturer:	Heckler & Koch
Type:	assault rifle
Calibre:	5.56mm
Cartridge:	5.56 x 45mm NATO
Length:	758–998mm (29.84–39.29in)
Length of barrel:	480mm (18.9in)
Number of grooves:	6
Weight:	3.43kg (7.54lb)
Cyclic rate of fire:	750rpm
Practical rate of fire:	200rpm
Operation:	gas
Magazine capacity:	30
Fire mode:	semi-, full-auto
Muzzle velocity:	920mps (3018fps)
Maximum range:	1000m (3280ft)
Effective range:	400m (1312ft)
Entered service:	1995

G36C

For some tactical missions, subcompact dimensions are still not handy enough, especially in the field of law enforcement. Aware of this, the designers and engineers at Heckler & Koch did their best to further minimize the already shortened G36K in both dimensions and weight. The result was the G36C, a weapon with the dimensions and firepower of a submachine gun, but with the penetration capabilities of the 5.56mm round. All parts – except barrel, forehand and folding buttstock – are modular and therefore exchangeable against those of other members of the G36 product family. Picatinny Rails for the bottom and both sides of the foregrip are also available to mount a variety of aiming devices, such as a red dot aiming system (which puts a red dot onto the target at the point where the bullet will strike). The four-prong flash hider is similar to the one mounted on the G36K, but is shorter in dimensions. The low-built Picatinny Rails with deeply integrated sights allow a flat line-of-sight. The mounting of any form of optical sights is easily possible. The G36C is an extremely reliable weapon, ideally suited to counter-terrorist and law-enforcement operations, where assault teams want weapons that are reliable, accurate, have full-automatic fire and good balance. The use of polymer materials helps to reduce weight.

SPECIFICATIONS

Manufacturer:	Heckler & Koch
Type:	close-quarter rifle
Calibre:	5.56mm
Cartridge:	5.56 x 45mm NATO
Length:	500–720mm (19.68–28.34in)
Length of barrel:	228mm (8.97in)
Number of grooves:	6
Weight:	2.8kg (6.16lb)
Cyclic rate of fire:	750rpm
Practical rate of fire:	200rpm
Operation:	gas
Magazine capacity:	30
Fire mode:	semi-, full-auto
Muzzle velocity:	850mps (2789fps)
Maximum range:	400m (1312ft)
Effective range:	100m (328ft)
Entered service:	1995

G36K

In 1995, in competition with designs from other manufacturers, the Heckler & Koch 50 was selected by the German Army as the successor to the G3 rifle. The rifle is now officially known as the Heckler & Koch *Gewehr* 36 – HK G36.

The G36 is available in four main versions, adapted to different roles. All versions share the same receiver, only the length and profile of the barrel and the length of the forearm and buttstock vary. The barrel, forearm and buttstock are easily replaced at unit level, thus four different weapons may be built around a single receiver.

The G36K (K for *Kurz*, meaning "short") is an assault rifle with a shortened forearm and barrel. The barrel is fitted with a large, four-prong flash hider in place of the vortex-type found on the other versions. The dimensions of the G36K make it especially suited for use by vehicle crews, special forces and law-enforcement entry units. Intermediate in size between the older HK33K and HK53 rifles, it lacks a bayonet lug and cannot fire rifle grenades. It may be fed from 100-round magazine drums if necessary, but it will not accept the bipod intended for the MG36 light support weapon (the bipod does fit, but it cannot be kept in a collapsed position). The G36K also accepts the 40mm grenade launcher.

SPECIFICATIONS

Manufacturer:	Heckler & Koch
Type:	assault rifle
Calibre:	5.56mm
Cartridge:	5.56 x 45mm NATO
Length:	615–858mm (24.21–33.77in)
Length of barrel:	320mm (13in)
Number of grooves:	6
Weight:	3.13kg (6.88lb)
Cyclic rate of fire:	750rpm
Practical rate of fire:	200rpm
Operation:	gas
Magazine capacity:	30 or 100
Fire mode:	semi-, full-auto
Muzzle velocity:	850mps (2789fps)
Maximum range:	400m (1312ft)
Effective range:	100m (328ft)
Entered service:	1995

HK PDW

Following a NATO panel enquiry into close combat and medium-range firefight scenarios, Heckler & Koch designed a new multi-role Personal Defence Weapon (PDW) in a new calibre – 4.6 x 30mm. The German company believes that the PDW is a perfect three-in-one solution: the firepower of a submachine gun, the medium-range capabilities of an assault rifle, and pistol-like close-combat dimensions.

Because of its low weight, small dimensions and less than half of the recoil of a normal 9 x 19mm submachine gun, the PDW has the handling features of a .22 weapon. It is extremely easy to operate and control and – due to the low recoil impulse of the ammunition – very steady during burst fire, with a firing rate of 950 rounds per minute.

The PDW has an integrated retractable buttstock, and ambidextrous cocking and decocking thanks to a centrally positioned cocking lever. The integrated Picatinny Rail allows the mounting of various optical sights. A folding fore-grip makes handling and control of the PDW easy during firing. The only drawback with the PDW is the calibre of the rounds it fires. The typical 9mm submachine gun round has good stopping power, whereas the 4.6mm bullet lacks the punch of the heavier bullet. Nevertheless, the PDW is an innovative step forward in submachine gun design.

SPECIFICATIONS

Manufacturer:	Heckler & Koch
Type:	submachine gun
Calibre:	4.6mm
Cartridge:	4.6 x 30mm
Length:	340–540mm (13.38–21.25in)
Length of barrel:	180mm (7in)
Number of grooves:	6
Weight:	1.5kg (3.3lb)
Cyclic rate of fire:	950rpm
Practical rate of fire:	200rpm
Operation:	gas
Magazine capacity:	20 or 40
Fire mode:	semi-, full-auto, three-round burst
Muzzle velocity:	375mps (1230fps)
Maximum range:	400m (1312ft)
Effective range:	200m (656ft)
Entered service:	1992

HK21

The HK21E (E for "Export") is a lightweight, general purpose machine gun in 7.62mm calibre. It can be fired from a tripod, bipod or from the shoulder (though accuracy suffers if the latter option is chosen). The HK21's closed-bolt operation and free-floating barrel provide excellent accuracy akin to a sniper rifle when using the bipod or tripod. With its cyclic rate of fire of 800 rounds per minute (13 rounds per second) the 21E can suppress a target area, but its superior accuracy allows it to be used in ways and in roles never before envisioned for a machine gun. The HK21E provides the user with a simple, quick-change barrel capability, and the Heckler & Koch design takes the convenience and ease of the barrel change to new levels of simplicity. To change the barrel the bolt is locked open, the barrel release lever depressed with the thumb and the barrel rotated 35 degrees, and removed rearward from the weapon using only one hand. This procedure can be easily accomplished even after firing 1000 rounds, because the well-insulated barrel handle precludes the need for an asbestos glove. A special insulated spare barrel carrier is available that allows a scalding-hot barrel slung across the shoulder to be safely carried by a member of the gun crew on the battlefield. The HK21 is without doubt one of the finest light machine guns in service today.

SPECIFICATIONS

Manufacturer:	*Heckler & Koch*
Type:	*light machine gun*
Calibre:	*7.62mm*
Cartridge:	*7.62 x 51mm NATO*
Length:	*1140mm (44.88in)*
Length of barrel:	*560mm (22in)*
Number of grooves:	*4*
Weight:	*9.3kg (20.46lb)*
Cyclic rate of fire:	*800rpm*
Practical rate of fire:	*300rpm*
Operation:	*delayed blowback*
Magazine capacity:	*metal link belt*
Fire mode:	*full-auto*
Muzzle velocity:	*840mps (2756fps)*
Maximum range:	*2000m (6561ft)*
Effective range:	*800m (2624ft)*
Entered service:	*1983*

HK33

The Heckler & Koch 33 rifle is essentially a scaled-down version of the G3 designed to accept the 5.56mm cartridge. The HK33E is the first 5.56 x 45-calibre rifle to use the delayed roller-lock bolt first perfected in the G3. In semi-automatic only mode for the American market the rifle is known as the HK93. The HK33 uses exactly the same trigger, bolt and firing mechanism as the G3, but is shorter and lighter. It also has the same sighting system and method of operation.

The most common version of the rifle is equipped with steel 25-round magazines, though recently steel 30-round magazines have been introduced by Heckler & Koch for the law-enforcement and military markets. The magazines themselves are extremely durable, and will usually work after having been run over by a vehicle. Most common variants are the HK33A2 and A3, i.e. fixed and retractable stock versions respectively. The E version normally has black furniture (as shown above), though it can be supplied in a camouflage pattern or in sand colour depending on user requirements. The HK33E is available with a fixed butt, with a sliding butt and in a sniping configuration.

The SG/1 version is the sniper variant, and has a cheek pad, fixed butt, bipod and telescopic sight. As with all Heckler & Koch weapons, it is very reliable.

SPECIFICATIONS

Manufacturer:	Heckler & Koch
Type:	assault rifle
Calibre:	5.56mm
Cartridge:	5.56 x 45mm NATO
Length:	675–865mm (26.57–34in)
Length of barrel:	322mm (12.67in)
Number of grooves:	6
Weight:	3.89kg (8.55lb)
Cyclic rate of fire:	650rpm
Practical rate of fire:	200rpm
Operation:	delayed blowback
Magazine capacity:	25
Fire mode:	semi-, full-auto, three-round burst
Muzzle velocity:	880mps (2887fps)
Maximum range:	1500m (4921ft)
Effective range:	550m (1804ft)
Entered service:	1985

HK53

Heckler & Koch firearms are among the most technologically and tactically advanced weapons in the world. Using its robust and reliable delayed blowback, roller-locked bolt system, the company developed the G3 assault rifle. From this weapon the firm further developed a variety of weapons designed to meet any tactical need.

The HK33E and HK53 are modifications of the delayed blowback, roller-locked bolt operating system in weapons firing the proven and popular 5.56 x 45mm round. Common throughout each weapon group is the ability to use many interchangeable assembly groups and components. This allows personnel to be fully trained on one weapon group, but also have the knowledge to operate the entire weapon system.

The HK53 is only 50mm (1.96in) longer than the 9mm MP5 submachine gun, and thus offers the compact size and handiness of a submachine gun combined with the increased range and hard-hitting firepower of the 5.56mm round. The HK53 has a straight-line buttstock and roller-locked bolt system, which gives good control in burst or sustained fire modes. The special four-prong flash hider eliminates muzzle flash. Though originally called a submachine gun, it is in fact a very compact carbine.

SPECIFICATIONS

Manufacturer:	Heckler & Koch
Type:	carbine
Calibre:	5.56mm
Cartridge:	5.56 x 45mm NATO
Length:	758–998mm (29.84–39.29in)
Length of barrel:	480mm (18.9in)
Number of grooves:	6
Weight:	3.43kg (7.54lb)
Cyclic rate of fire:	750rpm
Practical rate of fire:	200rpm
Operation:	gas
Magazine capacity:	30
Fire mode:	semi-auto, full-auto
Muzzle velocity:	920mps (3018fps)
Maximum range:	1000m (3280ft)
Effective range:	400m (1312ft)
Entered service:	1973

MG36

The MG36 is identical in length to the G36 rifle, but the barrel is heavier and has a folding bipod. Normally 100-round magazine drums are used, but the weapon may also be fed from standard G36 box magazines. The low mass of the bolt and ergonomic in-line relationship of the barrel and the buttstock result in a highly controllable weapon when fired on full-automatic. The G36's gas system does not direct fouling gases back into the weapon's interior like conventional gas-operated rifles, which ensures reliable operation even after firing more than 15,000 rounds without cleaning. In addition, the polymer components can easily be cleaned with water.

The MG36 has a number of ambidextrous features to facilitate left- and right-hand firing: a safety/selector lever allows for easy actuation without adjusting the firing grip, the cocking lever doubles as a forward assist and can be used to chamber a round silently, and there is an ambidextrous bolt catch button. The bolt catch itself holds the bolt to the rear on the last round fired, and can be disabled by the shooter without tools, allowing the bolt to close when the magazine is fired empty.

The MG36 has a flash hider on the muzzle, which is shaped for grenade launching. The prominent carrying handle incorporates a sight.

SPECIFICATIONS

Manufacturer:	Heckler & Koch
Type:	light support weapon
Calibre:	5.56mm
Cartridge:	5.56 x 45mm NATO
Length:	760–990mm (29.92–38.98in)
Length of barrel:	622mm (24.5in)
Number of grooves:	4
Weight:	6.85kg (15.07lb)
Cyclic rate of fire:	600rpm
Practical rate of fire:	200rpm
Operation:	gas
Magazine capacity:	30 or 100
Fire mode:	semi-, full-auto
Muzzle velocity:	762mps (2500fps)
Maximum range:	1500m (4921ft)
Effective range:	400m (1312ft)
Entered service:	1995

MP5A2

The MP5 submachine gun is the undisputed choice of the vast majority of law-enforcement special response teams and military special operations units throughout the Western world. This is because the weapon is very reliable due to the fact that it fires from a closed bolt. In the firing position, inclined surfaces on the locking piece within the bolt carrier lie between the two rollers on the bolt head and force them out into recesses in the barrel extension. After ignition, the rollers are cammed inward against the locking piece's inclined planes by rearward pressure on the bolt head. The bolt carrier's rearward velocity is four times that of the bolt head. After the bolt carrier has moved to the rear 4mm (0.15in), the rollers on the bolt head are completely in, pressure has dropped to the required levels of safety, and the two parts continue their backward movement together. To further improve reliability, several years ago the MP5's bolt head was improved and strengthened to inhibit cracking.

The MP5A2 variant is fitted with a fixed buttstock. All MP5 stocks, except those designed for the shortened MP5K series, are interchangeable. Although the fixed buttstock provides the most stable firing platform, the MP5's retractable stock is among the finest in the world, and all in all the MP5 is a superb weapon.

SPECIFICATIONS

Manufacturer:	Heckler & Koch
Type:	submachine gun
Calibre:	9mm
Cartridge:	9mm Parabellum
Length:	680mm (26.7in)
Length of barrel:	225mm (8.86in)
Number of grooves:	6
Weight:	2.55kg (5.61lb)
Cyclic rate of fire:	800rpm
Practical rate of fire:	200rpm
Operation:	delayed blowback
Magazine capacity:	15 or 30
Fire mode:	semi-, full-auto, three-round burst
Muzzle velocity:	400mps (1312fps)
Maximum range:	200m (656ft)
Effective range:	100m (328ft)
Entered service:	1964

MP5A3

Because it fires from a closed, locked breech instead of utilizing the unlocked, open-bolt concept of most submachine guns, the MP5 is technically a "machine carbine" rather than a true submachine gun. That said, its compact size in comparison to assault rifles and the fact that it fires a pistol cartridge places it firmly in the submachine gun category. Firing from a closed bolt eliminates the "lurch" experienced with conventional open-bolt submachine guns when the trigger is pressed. From a user's point of view this allows easier and more accurate firing of the weapon, which endears the MP5 to hostage-rescue teams who require great accuracy when firing at terrorists in close proximity to hostages. Critics of the closed-bolt concept point to the increased residual heat build-up that results from a closed bolt, which can cause "cook-offs". However, because Heckler & Koch weapons are so well engineered this is an almost insignificant disadvantage.

The A3 version differs from the A2 version by having a single metal strut stock which can be slid forward to reduce the overall length of the weapon. There is a safety/selector lever above the trigger, with a choice of fire modes being semi-automatic, full-automatic and three-round burst. As well as iron sights, the MP5 range of submachine guns can be fitted with image intensifiers and aiming projectors.

SPECIFICATIONS

Manufacturer:	Heckler & Koch
Type:	submachine gun
Calibre:	9mm
Cartridge:	9mm Parabellum
Length:	490–660mm (19.3–26in)
Length of barrel:	225mm (8.86in)
Number of grooves:	6
Weight:	2.55kg (5.61lb)
Cyclic rate of fire:	800rpm
Practical rate of fire:	200rpm
Operation:	delayed blowback
Magazine capacity:	15 or 30
Fire mode:	semi-, full-auto, three-round burst
Muzzle velocity:	400mps (1312fps)
Maximum range:	200m (656ft)
Effective range:	100m (328ft)
Entered service:	1964

MP5K

The MP5K is the ultimate close-quarters weapon. At 2kg (4.4lb) and less than 330mm (13in) long, the MP5K is easily concealed and carried and is ideal for police and counter-terrorist use. All MP5Ks can be fitted with an optional folding buttstock, and it can also be fired from inside a specially designed briefcase.

Apart from a shorter barrel and smaller 15-round magazine, the K version (K meaning *Kurz* or short) is mechanically identical to the full-sized MP5. The MP5 series is excellent for counter-terrorist work but is less suited to general use in the field. There are two main reasons for this. First, the precision engineering required to produce Heckler & Koch submachine guns makes each gun relatively expensive (this is a definite move away from the "cheap and cheerful" submachine guns mass-produced during World War II). Second, while they are reliable weapons, they do require great care and attention to keep them fully functional. They are too well made to tolerate extended combat use in sand, mud or snow.

The MP5K is used by undercover operatives because it is easy to conceal in clothing and bags. In addition, it is an excellent weapon for plainclothes soldiers working in unmarked cars, who often require a high-volume-of-fire weapon on operations.

SPECIFICATIONS

Manufacturer:	*Heckler & Koch*
Type:	*shortened submachine gun*
Calibre:	*9mm*
Cartridge:	*9mm Parabellum*
Length:	*325mm (12.8in)*
Length of barrel:	*115mm (4.52in)*
Number of grooves:	*6*
Weight:	*2kg (4.4lb)*
Cyclic rate of fire:	*900rpm*
Practical rate of fire:	*200rpm*
Operation:	*delayed blowback*
Magazine capacity:	*15 or 30*
Fire mode:	*semi-, full-auto, three-round burst*
Muzzle velocity:	*375mps (1230fps)*
Maximum range:	*150m (492ft)*
Effective range:	*50m (164ft)*
Entered service:	*1976*

MP5K PDW

This weapon is based on the shortened MP5K sub-machine gun with the addition of a side-folding stock and a muzzle flash hider. It is designed for use by troops who would normally travel in cramped vehicles or aircraft, such as tanks or helicopters. When folded, it is small enough to fit under a car seat.

The Personal Defence Weapon (PDW) is a compact weapon whose chassis, detachable foregrip and folding stock are constructed primarily from injection-moulded polymer, thus saving weight without compromising durability. The trigger, front and rear sights, bolt handle, fire selector, magazine release, sling swivel, butt plate and retaining pins are all metal, with the barrel itself made of brass. The ambidextrous fire-selector lever is on either side of the trigger unit. The stock is almost as long as the rest of the gun, and when extended it makes the gun long enough to fire from the shoulder to increase overall accuracy.

As stated above, the sights are made of metal; the front is a blade sight with a protective shroud, while the rear is a turret sight with different apertures for different ranges. There are three lugs on the barrel for the attachment of a silencer or grenade launcher. The butt may be removed and replaced by a cap on the receiver. There is an optional two- or three-round burst facility.

SPECIFICATIONS

Manufacturer:	*Heckler & Koch*
Type:	*special forces submachine gun*
Calibre:	*9mm*
Cartridge:	*9mm Parabellum*
Length:	*368–800mm (14.48–31.5in)*
Length of barrel:	*140mm (5.5in)*
Number of grooves:	*6*
Weight:	*2.79kg (6.13lb)*
Cyclic rate of fire:	*900rpm*
Practical rate of fire:	*200rpm*
Operation:	*delayed blowback*
Magazine capacity:	*15 or 30*
Fire mode:	*semi-, full-auto, three-round burst*
Muzzle velocity:	*375mps (1230fps)*
Maximum range:	*150m (492ft)*
Effective range:	*50m (164ft)*
Entered service:	*1992*

MP5N

Developed especially for one of America's most élite special operations troops, the US Navy Sea-Air-Land (SEAL) teams, the MP5 "Navy" model comes with an ambidextrous trigger group and threaded barrel as standard. There are also a number of accessories that can be attached to the MP5 to enhance performance in low-light conditions. The UITC Night Stalker/SO laser aiming module, for example, is a modular laser aiming device that can be mounted on a variety of firearms. This law-enforcement module contains two laser diodes and an infrared flashlight for use with night-vision equipment. The Night Stalker/SO offers the option of dual visible or dual infrared lasers which can be configured for long- and short-range settings. Both may be independently adjusted.

The Night Stalker/SO has recessed control buttons which control each sighting system separately, and have no exposed wires. The controls and quick release levers are on both sides, thus allowing for fully ambidextrous operation of the unit. Operation involves first selecting the desired laser by switching the appropriate button. The laser can then be activated by touching the activation pad. Laser blink rates may be programmed for identification purposes.

The MP5N has a collapsible stock for use in confined spaces and ease of carrying.

SPECIFICATIONS

Manufacturer:	*Heckler & Koch*
Type:	*special forces submachine gun*
Calibre:	*9mm*
Cartridge:	*9mm Parabellum*
Length:	*610–781mm (24–30.75in)*
Length of barrel:	*225mm (8.86in)*
Number of grooves:	*6*
Weight:	*3.5kg (7.7lb)*
Cyclic rate of fire:	*800rpm*
Practical rate of fire:	*200rpm*
Operation:	*delayed blowback*
Magazine capacity:	*15 or 30*
Fire mode:	*semi-, full-auto, three-round burst*
Muzzle velocity:	*283mps (928fps)*
Maximum range:	*150m (492ft)*
Effective range:	*50m (164ft)*
Entered service:	*unknown*

MP5SD

This weapon was developed for specialized applications requiring fully realized sound and flash suppression. The removable sound suppressor is integrated into the weapon's design and conforms to the normal length and profile of a conventional, unsuppressed submachine gun. The MP5SD uses an integral aluminium or optional wet technology stainless steel sound suppressor, and does not require use of subsonic ammunition for sound reduction.

Common throughout the MP5 range of weapons is the ability to use many interchangeable assembly groups and components. This provides the ability to train personnel within one weapon group and have them competent with the entire weapon system. The SD version is no different.

Heckler & Koch scope mounts can be attached to the SD without tools at special points. They ensure 100 percent return to zero and do not interfere with the use of the weapon's iron sights.

The SD1 variant has a receiver end cap and no buttstock; the SD2 variant has a fixed buttstock; the SD3 variant has a folding butt; the SD4 variant is as the D1 version with an added three-round burst facility; the SD5 is as the D2 version but with an added three-round burst facility; and the SD6 variant resembles the D3 version with an added three-round burst facility.

SPECIFICATIONS

Manufacturer:	*Heckler & Koch*
Type:	*silenced submachine gun*
Calibre:	*9mm*
Cartridge:	*9mm Parabellum*
Length:	*550mm (21.65in)*
Length of barrel:	*146mm (5.75in)*
Number of grooves:	*6*
Weight:	*2.8kg (6.16lb)*
Cyclic rate of fire:	*800rpm*
Practical rate of fire:	*200rpm*
Operation:	*delayed blowback*
Magazine capacity:	*15 or 30*
Fire mode:	*semi-, full-auto, three-round burst*
Muzzle velocity:	*285mps (935fps)*
Maximum range:	*200m (656ft)*
Effective range:	*100m (328ft)*
Entered service:	*1975*

MP5SF

The MP5SF (single fire) carbine is a semi-automatic only variant of the MP5 fitted with a trigger group that prevents full-automatic firing. It is an ideal squad vehicle carbine and is an excellent supplement or replacement for a police shotgun. It has less recoil, greater range and more ammunition capacity than a shotgun and is especially suitable for small-stature officers. It is used by military and law enforcement in 50 countries. This selective-fire weapon can be shouldered or hand-fired.

The unique features of the Heckler & Koch MP5 range of submachine guns include a free-floating cold hammer-forged barrel, stamped sheet steel receiver, fluted chamber, straight-line stock and a pistol grip with ambidextrous safety/selector lever. The bare metal surfaces of the MP5 are phosphated and coated with a black lacquer paint. This dry lacquer coating is applied with a magnetic charge and then baked onto the metal in an oven. The resulting finish is highly resistant to salt water corrosion and surface wear.

Another variant of the MP5 aimed at the law-enforcement market is the MP5/10, which is chambered for the 10mm Auto cartridge and has a carbon-fibre, reinforced straight-box magazine. It also has a dual magazine clamp to allow two magazines to be attached and rapidly switched into the firing position.

SPECIFICATIONS

Manufacturer:	Heckler & Koch
Type:	submachine gun
Calibre:	9mm
Cartridge:	9mm Parabellum
Length:	680mm (26.7in)
Length of barrel:	225mm (8.86in)
Number of grooves:	6
Weight:	2.55kg (5.61lb)
Cyclic rate of fire:	800rpm
Practical rate of fire:	200rpm
Operation:	delayed blowback
Magazine capacity:	15 or 30
Fire mode:	semi-, full-auto, three-round burst
Muzzle velocity:	400mps (1312fps)
Maximum range:	200m (656ft)
Effective range:	100m (328ft)
Entered service:	1964

MSG90

The MSG90 bears a close resemblance to the G3 assault rifle. It is a magazine-fed, semi-automatic rifle chambered for the NATO-standardized 7.62 x 51mm cartridge. Like most Heckler & Koch rifles and submachine guns, it uses the delayed blowback, roller-locked bolt operating system that delivers excellent accuracy and reliable performance. Most of the rifle's internal components, plus its stock, magazine and fire-control mechanism, are interchangeable with those of the G3.

The MSG90 also incorporates a number of features pertinent to a dedicated sniper rifle. For example, reinforcing ribs are welded onto both sides of the receiver directly over the slide rails, which enhance the receiver's structural integrity and lend support to the barrel/receiver interface. For quiet loading, the MSG90's receiver is equipped with a forward assist. The absence of fixed sights on the MSG90 further indicates the specialized role that it is designed to fulfil.

Another salient feature of the MSG90 is the push-pinned trigger housing. By first removing the stock, the shooter can quickly replace the semi-automatic trigger group and housing with a unit that facilitates full-automatic firing. Essentially, the MSG90 differs from the PSG-1 in its ability to be deployed as a support weapon.

SPECIFICATIONS

Manufacturer:	Heckler & Koch
Type:	sniper rifle
Calibre:	7.62mm
Cartridge:	7.62 x 51mm NATO
Length:	1165mm (45.87in)
Length of barrel:	600mm (23.62in)
Number of grooves:	4
Weight:	6.4kg (14.08lb)
Cyclic rate of fire:	n/a
Practical rate of fire:	20rpm
Operation:	delayed blowback
Magazine capacity:	5 or 20
Fire mode:	semi-, full-auto
Muzzle velocity:	820mps (2690fps)
Maximum range:	1800m (5905ft)
Effective range:	450m (1476ft)
Entered service:	1987

PSG-1

The PSG-1 is one of the most accurate semi-automatic sniper rifles in the world. The accuracy standard that all PSG-1s must meet is 50 rounds of match ammunition into an 80mm (3.149in) circle at a range of 300m (984ft). The PSG-1 is popular with special operations units and anti-terrorist squads. However, it is unsuited to military operations in the field for two reasons. First, it ejects the shells about 10m (32.8ft), which can easily give away a sniper's position. Second, it only can be fitted with the Hensoldt 6 x 42 sight. No other sight can be used, and the sight is only set up to be used up to a range of 600m (1968ft). Unfortunately that distance is the start of the optimal engagement range for military snipers.

With a heavy, free-floating barrel, adjustable butt, hand rest and its telescopic sight, the PSG-1 is an outstanding police sharpshooter weapon, though it is very expensive. The rifle has a system for silent bolt closing, and the trigger has an adjustable shoe to change its width to suit individual preferences. The barrel has a polygonal bore, which prevents the escape of the tiny quantities of gas that normally leak past the bullet in conventional firing. This means that the round's trajectory remains true after firing.

The PSG-1 is in use with the German anti-terrorist unit GSG 9, plus other police units around the world.

SPECIFICATIONS

Manufacturer:	*Heckler & Koch*
Type:	*sniper rifle*
Calibre:	*7.62mm*
Cartridge:	*7.62 x 51mm NATO*
Length:	*1208mm (47.56in)*
Length of barrel:	*650mm (25.6in)*
Number of grooves:	*4*
Weight:	*8.1kg (17.82lb)*
Cyclic rate of fire:	*n/a*
Practical rate of fire:	*15rpm*
Operation:	*delayed blowback*
Magazine capacity:	*5 or 20*
Fire mode:	*semi-auto*
Muzzle velocity:	*830mps (2723ft)*
Maximum range:	*600m (1968ft)*
Effective range:	*400m (1312ft)*
Entered service:	*1985*

UMP

The German firm Heckler & Koch have long dominated the marked for submachine guns with their MP5 models, and quite rightly. This design is, though, now over three decades old and so the company has for over a decade worked on the design of a new submachine gun which it hopes will prove to be just as popular as the MP5. The UMP 45 (Universal Machine Pistol calibre .45) is the final product of this development, and it does indeed look as though it will be as successful as the MP5 series.

The entire stock is made from polymer, giving the gun high strength but low weight. The buttstock can be folded onto the right side of the gun, and the whole weapon is very stable and solid to fire. Instead of the MP5's roller-delayed action, the gun has a simple blowback action and it fires from a closed bolt. Several trigger options are available, including two-round burst.

The most surprising item is the calibre: the UMP fires the .45 ACP (Automatic Colt Pistol) cartridge, and not the 9mm as used in other submachine guns. A variety of different accessories is available, including a sling, a vertical foregrip, silencers, sights and lamps. The UMP45 is delivered with a 25-round magazine as standard, but 10-round magazines are also available.

SPECIFICATIONS

Manufacturer:	Heckler & Koch
Type:	submachine gun
Calibre:	.45in
Cartridge:	45 ACP
Length:	442–675mm (17.7–27in)
Length of barrel:	200mm (7.87in)
Number of grooves:	unknown
Weight:	unknown
Cyclic rate of fire:	700rpm
Practical rate of fire:	200rpm
Operation:	blowback
Magazine capacity:	25 or 10
Fire mode:	semi-, full-auto, two-round burst
Muzzle velocity:	442mps (1450fps)
Maximum range:	200m (656ft)
Effective range:	100m (328ft)
Entered service:	not yet in service

L7A2

The British General Purpose Machine Gun (GPMG) is a successful development of the Belgian FN MAG machine gun. The GPMG can be used in the light role, but is more normally used in the sustained-fire role, being mounted on a tripod with the C2 optical sight unit. A two-man team operates the weapon, and a number of weapons are normally grouped in a specialist machine-gun platoon. The L7A2 differs in several minor, but significant, ways from the FN weapon. The gas regulator, for example, has 10 positions (the minimum rate of fire is obtained at adjustment notch "8"), the bipod legs are adjustable for height, the buttstock is made of plastic, the gas cylinder permits installation of a heavy barrel, the chrome bore plating is thicker, the sear has two bents to engage a special piston extension (for safety when cocking, should it slip accidentally from the operator's hand), and the cartridge guide pawl is a two-piece component.

Sturdy, reliable and very accurate, the L7A2 is undoubtedly the best GPMG ever fielded and has served the British Army well for over 40 years. Used on a tripod the GPMG is effective up to a range of 1800m (5905ft), though it is difficult to spot strike at this range because the tracer rounds in the ammunition belt usually burn out at a range of 1100m (3608ft).

SPECIFICATIONS

Manufacturer:	*Royal Small Arms*
Type:	*general purpose machine gun*
Calibre:	*7.62mm*
Cartridge:	*7.62 x 51mm NATO*
Length:	*1232mm (48.5in)*
Length of barrel:	*679mm (26.75in)*
Number of grooves:	*4*
Weight:	*10.9kg (23.98lb)*
Cyclic rate of fire:	*800rpm*
Practical rate of fire:	*300rpm*
Operation:	*gas*
Magazine capacity:	*metal link belt*
Fire mode:	*full-auto*
Muzzle velocity:	*838mps (2750fps)*
Maximum range:	*3500m (1148ft)*
Effective range:	*1800m (5905ft)*
Entered service:	*1963*

L86

The L86A1 Light Support Weapon (LSW) is essentially a version of the SA80 assault rifle with a longer barrel and bipod fitted on an outrigger, as well as a rear grip. The trigger has been redesigned twice, and the push button, cross-bolt safety catch has been made stiffer to operate compared to early SA80s, to prevent it being accidentally knocked into the "on" position.

As the LSW uses rotary locking, virtually no dirt ingresses the action of the gun. In addition, the bore is chrome-lined, thus cleaning in the field is fairly straightforward. That said, dirt can accumulate in the weapon through the holes in the receiver, which can present problems on the battlefield.

The recoil is very much less than with heavier-calibre weapons, which helps in recruit training and minimizes weapon movement when firing. The LSW is gas-operated, self-loading and magazine-fed with the facility for single-shot or full-automatic fire. In addition, the strength of construction enables muzzle launching of 21mm grenades. A great advantage for infantrymen is that the magazines for the SA80 and LSW are interchangeable. In addition, around 80 percent of LSW parts are interchangeable with the SA80. Each British eight-man infantry section is usually equipped with two LSWs for support.

SPECIFICATIONS

Manufacturer:	Royal Ordnance
Type:	light support weapon
Calibre:	5.56mm
Cartridge:	5.56 x 45mm NATO
Length:	900m (35.43in)
Length of barrel:	646mm (25.43in)
Number of grooves:	6
Weight:	6.1kg (13.42lb)
Cyclic rate of fire:	700rpm
Practical rate of fire:	200rpm
Operation:	gas
Magazine capacity:	30
Fire mode:	semi-, full-auto
Muzzle velocity:	970mps (3182fps)
Maximum range:	1500m (4921ft)
Effective range:	400m (1312ft)
Entered service:	1986

L96A1

The L96A1 has a plastic stock, a light bipod and a monopod in the butt, which allows the rifle to be laid on the target for long periods without the firer having to support the weight of the weapon. The A1 bipod is of the highest quality and mounts via a quick detachable fitting, integral with the fore-end. This system has five degrees of left and right cant built into the mount, resulting in enough movement so that the rifle can be supported in a level firing position on uneven surfaces. The bipod itself has a tension-adjustable ball joint, which allows tracking of moving targets without movement of the bipod feet. The legs of the bipod are spring loaded and positively lock into each height-adjustment notch. The skid-type feet of the bipod work well on any number of surfaces.

Originally designed for the British military in the early 1980s and designated the L96A1, the rifle was upgraded in the late 1980s to enhance its reliability in arctic weather conditions. This newly modified rifle received the designation Arctic Warfare (AW) model, though it also performs well in hot, humid climates. The AW is built to military requirements, and can fire 25,000 rounds before failure. The bolt body is partially covered with shallow fluting to allow space for debris to accumulate without binding or jamming the bolt.

SPECIFICATIONS

Manufacturer:	Accuracy International
Type:	sniper rifle
Calibre:	7.62mm
Cartridge:	7.62 x 51mm NATO
Length:	1194mm (47in)
Length of barrel:	655mm (25.6in)
Number of grooves:	4
Weight:	6.5kg (14.3lb)
Cyclic rate of fire:	n/a
Practical rate of fire:	10rpm
Operation:	bolt
Magazine capacity:	10
Fire mode:	single shot
Muzzle velocity:	850mps (2788fps)
Maximum range:	3000m (9842ft)
Effective range:	1000m (3280ft)
Entered service:	1985

SA80

The SA80 is the standard assault rifle of the British Army. Despite its bullpup design, standard adjustable optical telescope and a pressed steel receiver, it has been plagued by problems from the beginning, and these problems persist. For example, in terms of overall reliability the SA80 does not perform well in field conditions, and in the 1991 Gulf War (the first operational deployment outside Northern Ireland) there were reports of sand clogging the trigger-mechanism housing and the gas regulator. When used in the jungles of Belize, the standard-issue British Army insect repellent melted the rifle's plastic furniture! Despite the problems, over 330,000 are in British service.

The weapon is of reasonably lightweight construction, having a pressed-steel receiver in which the bolt rides upon guide rods. This has certainly reduced manufacturing time, but has had the unfortunate result of creating a somewhat fragile weapon. The SA80's sight is the Sight Unit Small Arms Trilux (SUSAT), a short telescope with an illuminated recticle which works well enough.

A version of the SA80 is the L86A1 cadet rifle, which has a manual bolt handle in place of the gas system and a carrying handle and flip aperture sight. It is restricted to Army Cadet Force training and can be fitted with a .22RF adaptor for indoor range shooting.

SPECIFICATIONS

Manufacturer:	Royal Ordnance
Type:	assault rifle
Calibre:	5.56mm
Cartridge:	5.56 x 45mm NATO
Length:	785mm (30.9in)
Length of barrel:	518mm (20.4in)
Number of grooves:	6
Weight:	3.81kg (8.38lb)
Cyclic rate of fire:	650–800rpm
Practical rate of fire:	150rpm
Operation:	gas
Magazine capacity:	30
Fire mode:	semi-, full-auto
Muzzle velocity:	940mps (3084fps)
Maximum range:	1000m (3280ft)
Effective range:	400m (1312ft)
Entered service:	1986

SUPER MAGNUM

The Accuracy International Super Magnum rifle is essentially an upgraded version of its L96A1 rifle, fitted and strengthened to fire high-powered magnum cartridges. The calibres it is available in are: 7mm Remington Magnum, .300 Winchester Magnum, and the .338 Lapua Magnum. Using the Lapua cartridge the Super Magnum is capable of approaching the range of some .5in-calibre sniper rifles.

This excellent bolt-action rifle is fed from a five-round detachable magazine, and the entire rifle is centred on a large aluminium frame, upon which the action and the barrel are mounted. At the front end of the frame, a Parker Hale bipod can be attached. The heavy, free-floating barrel is supported by an aluminium frame, and the whole assembly is held in a high-impact plastic stock. To help control any muzzle jump, the barrel and butt are in a straight line, with the butt length being adjustable by the addition or removal of extension pieces.

The rifle is set up to accept a variety of scopes through a one-piece scope mount. At the end of the barrel a large muzzle brake is attached, and the heavy barrel gives the rifle excellent accuracy. The rifle is already in the service of the Netherlands as a counter-sniper weapon, and several other armies are evaluating it.

SPECIFICATIONS

Manufacturer:	*Accuracy International*
Type:	*sniper rifle*
Calibre:	*7mm, .300in, .338in*
Cartridge:	*various*
Length:	*1255mm (50in)*
Length of barrel:	*67.77mm (27in)*
Number of grooves:	*4*
Weight:	*6.8kg (14.96lb)*
Cyclic rate of fire:	*n/a*
Practical rate of fire:	*5rpm*
Operation:	*bolt*
Magazine capacity:	*5*
Fire mode:	*single shot*
Muzzle velocity:	*850mps (2788fps)*
Maximum range:	*3000m (9842ft)*
Effective range:	*1100m (3609ft)*
Entered service:	*2000*

GALIL

Following the Six-Day War of 1967, there were calls among the Israeli military for a lighter and handier individual weapon than the FN FAL, which was then in Israeli service. A design team led by Israel Galil tested a variety of rifles, including the AK-47, M16 and Stoner 63. It reached the conclusion that it liked the 5.56mm cartridge of the M16, but preferred the AK-47's conventional piston to the M16's direct-impingement gas system. It therefore selected one of the most up-to-date variants of the AK-47 from which to work: the Valmet M62. The Finnish firm provided the first 1000 receivers for the new rifle, which was officially adopted in 1972 and called the Galil. Insufficient quantities of the Galil were available at the time of the 1973 Yom Kippur War, so Israel was provided with large quantities of US M16 rifles.

The Galil's long magazine requires long bipod legs. These are suspended from a large casting that incorporates the gas cylinder, front sight base and front sling attachment staple. The bipod is equipped with a wire cutter that uses the bipod legs for leverage. The Galil's plastic pistol grip is very functional and was taken from the Hungarian AKM/AMD-65 rifles. Its sharp bottom flare prevents the hand from slipping, and the grip has been mounted to the receiver at precisely the correct grip-to-frame angle.

SPECIFICATIONS

Manufacturer:	Israel Military Industries
Type:	assault rifle
Calibre:	7.62mm
Cartridge:	7.62 x 51mm NATO
Length:	810–1050mm (31.89–41.34in)
Length of barrel:	535mm (21in)
Number of grooves:	4
Weight:	4.4kg (9.68lb)
Cyclic rate of fire:	650rpm
Practical rate of fire:	150rpm
Operation:	gas
Magazine capacity:	25
Fire mode:	semi-, full-auto
Muzzle velocity:	850mps (2788fps)
Maximum range:	1000m (3280ft)
Effective range:	400m (1312ft)
Entered service:	1972

GALIL SNIPER

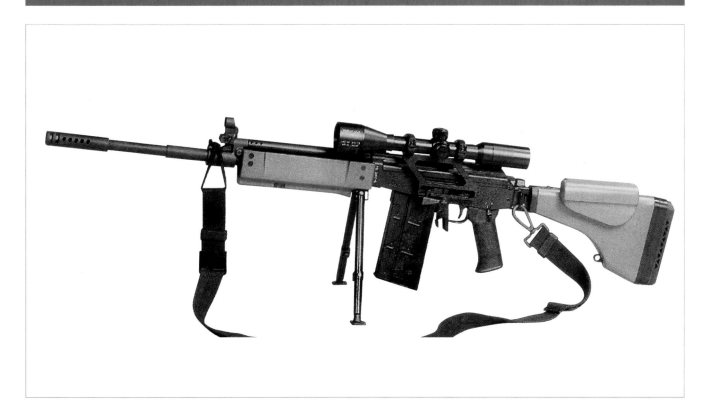

The Galil 7.62mm sniping rifle was introduced by Israel Military Industries (IMI) in 1983. It was developed by the Israel Defence Force (IDF) to provide an extremely accurate sniping rifle while at the same time being very robust. It has the basic Galil rifle mechanism in 7.62mm calibre, but with special features.

The bipod is mounted on the fore-end, close to the receiver where it can be easily adjusted by the firer, and the barrel is heavier than standard. The telescope sight mount is on the side of the receiver and can be mounted and dismounted without disturbing the zeroing (a Nimrod 6 x 40 telescope sight is provided as standard).

The butt folds for ease of convenience in storage and transport, and the cheek piece and recoil pad are both adjustable. The barrel is fitted with a combined compensator and muzzle brake, which can be removed and replaced by a silencer, for which subsonic ammunition is provided. The rifle has a two-stage trigger, and the mechanism has been altered so that only semi-automatic fire will work. The standard iron sights are retained for emergency use.

The Galil is a very robust weapon: models have been buried in sand, immersed in water, driven over by trucks and generally mistreated before firing hundreds of rounds without any problems.

SPECIFICATIONS

Manufacturer:	Israel Military Industries
Type:	sniper rifle
Calibre:	7.62mm
Cartridge:	7.62 x 51mm NATO
Length:	840–1115mm (33–43.9in)
Length of barrel:	508mm (20in)
Number of grooves:	4
Weight:	6.4kg (14.08lb)
Cyclic rate of fire:	n/a
Practical rate of fire:	10rpm
Operation:	gas
Magazine capacity:	30
Fire mode:	semi-auto
Muzzle velocity:	815mps (2674fps)
Maximum range:	2000m (6561ft)
Effective range:	800m (2624ft)
Entered service:	1983

MICRO UZI

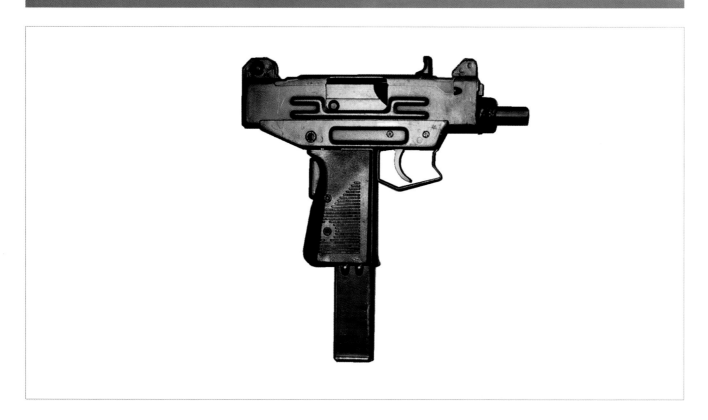

The Uzi family of submachine guns is only in limited use in Israel. The models in service are the Mini Uzi and Micro Uzi, which are mainly being used by the rappelling and fast-roping sections of counter-terrorist units. These units need a compact gun to allow them ease of movement in tight spaces, yet require a more powerful weapon than the average handgun.

The Micro Uzi has four main users in Israel: counter-terrorist units; high-ranking officers who consider it as a status symbol and want to be armed with a distinctive "combat" weapon, but not with a clumsy big and long assault rifle; Unit 669, consisting of airborne doctors and medics; and air crew personnel, especially in helicopters, since the Micro Uzi has greater firepower than a handgun, yet is in a compact and handy frame.

There are three Micro Uzi versions in use in Israel: the standard Micro Uzi, Counter-Terrorist Micro Uzi and the new Para Uzi, all of which are closed-bolt weapons.

These Counter-Terrorist and Para modified weapons have several important improvements compared to the standard version: illuminated night sights; an enlarged front and back sights block, which enables a faster target acquisition; threads along the barrel for mounting suppressors; and a cocking handle on the right side of the weapon.

SPECIFICATIONS

Manufacturer:	*Israel Military Industries*
Type:	*compact submachine gun*
Calibre:	*9mm*
Cartridge:	*9mm Parabellum*
Length:	*250–460mm (9.84–18.11in)*
Length of barrel:	*117mm (4.61in)*
Number of grooves:	*4*
Weight:	*1.95kg (4.29lb)*
Cyclic rate of fire:	*1250rpm*
Practical rate of fire:	*250rpm*
Operation:	*blowback*
Magazine capacity:	*20*
Fire mode:	*semi-, full-auto*
Muzzle velocity:	*330mps (1082fps)*
Maximum range:	*200m (656ft)*
Effective range:	*30m (98ft)*
Entered service:	*1982*

MINI UZI

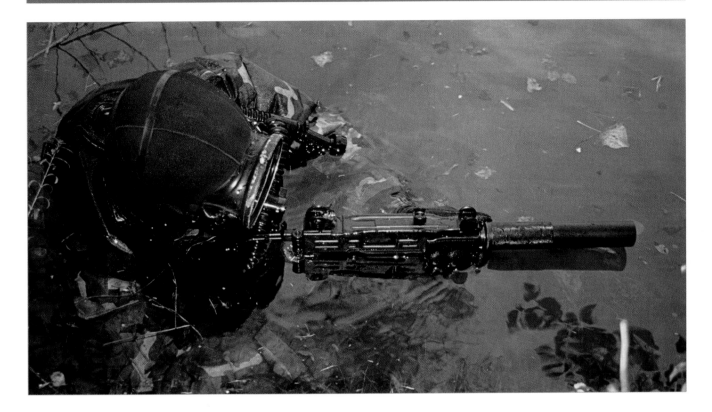

The Mini Uzi is similar to the standard Uzi but is more compact and actually has a higher rate of fire (this has aroused criticism because the higher rate of fire makes the weapon harder to control when burst-firing). The Mini Uzi can be fired from an open bolt or a closed bolt and, like the standard Uzi, uses a blowback operation (whereby the breech is kept closed by the inertia of the breechblock and pressure of the recoil spring, so that, on firing, the chamber pressure "blows the bolt back" once it overcomes this inertia). The smaller size of the Mini Uzi allows it to be used easily in small, enclosed confines, such as the inside of an armoured personnel carrier.

The Mini-Uzi has a folding stock for easier concealability, and is considered an excellent weapon due to its small size and reliability. The magazine for the Mini Uzi and the standard Uzi are the same (though the Mini can also use special short magazines), and some of the parts between the two weapons are also interchangeable. The Mini Uzi has a simple wire folding stock, and has compensating slots cut into the top of the muzzle.

Some modified Micro Uzis (see page 54) are fitted with the Mini Uzi's stock, which is bigger and much more comfortable than the original Micro Uzi one. All in all, the Mini Uzi is an excellent submachine gun.

SPECIFICATIONS

Manufacturer:	Israel Military Industries
Type:	compact submachine gun
Calibre:	9mm
Cartridge:	9mm Parabellum
Length:	360–600mm (14.17–23.62in)
Length of barrel:	197mm (7.75in)
Number of grooves:	4
Weight:	2.7kg (5.94lb)
Cyclic rate of fire:	950rpm
Practical rate of fire:	200rpm
Operation:	blowback
Magazine capacity:	20, 25 or 32
Fire mode:	semi-, full-auto
Muzzle velocity:	352mps (1155fps)
Maximum range:	150m (656ft)
Effective range:	70m (230ft)
Entered service:	1981

NEGREV

The Negev light machine gun was developed in the late 1980s with the operational needs and specifications of the Israel Defence Force (IDF) in mind. It was designed to replace all current light machine guns in use with the IDF on all the relevant platforms: infantry, vehicle, airborne and maritime.

On the surface the Negev looks suspiciously like the Minimi, and the Israeli weapon is very close in concept to the Belgian gun. Internally, though, the two firearms vary in several technical aspects. All in all, both items are very much alike, being very accurate, reliable and lightweight. Based on IDF operational experience with both weapons over the years in adverse field conditions, the Negev proved itself to be more reliable in harsh desert conditions than the Minimi. The Negev's folding metal stock is also a big advantage over the Minimi.

The Negev is an air-cooled weapon with a rotating bolt. The mechanism uses a conventional gas and piston method of operating, with a two-piece rotary bolt. The Negev can fire from either a magazine (either Galil or M16 box magazines) or from a belt with an adapter fitted in place. The assault machine gun version has the same receiver, pistol grip and butt, but has no bipod and a shorter barrel. The Negev is a very sturdy weapon.

SPECIFICATIONS

Manufacturer:	Israel Military Industries
Type:	light machine gun
Calibre:	5.56mm
Cartridge:	5.56 x 45mm NATO
Length:	780–1020mm (30.7–40.15in)
Length of barrel:	460mm (18.11in)
Number of grooves:	6
Weight:	7.5kg (16.5lb)
Cyclic rate of fire:	850–1000rpm
Practical rate of fire:	200rpm
Operation:	gas
Magazine capacity:	30, 35 or link belt
Fire mode:	semi-, full-auto
Muzzle velocity:	1000mps (3280fps)
Maximum range:	1500m (4921ft)
Effective range:	400m (1312ft)
Entered service:	1990

UZI

The Uzi, one of the most famous submachine guns in the world, is a compact weapon that has a square outline and is made from steel pressings riveted and spot-welded together. It uses a blowback mechanism, but has a bolt that actually wraps around the end of the barrel. The bolt face and firing pin are some 95mm (3.75in) back from the front edge of the bolt, the rest of which surrounds the chamber and rear of the barrel. Slots are cut into the bolt to allow empty cases to pass through when being ejected. By employing this wrap-around method a large bolt can be made that takes up little space. The return spring sits around a guide rod above the level of the barrel, which extends forward of the chamber.

The large pistol grip extends beneath the centre of the body, with the trigger assembly in front of this. The ammunition feed is actually through the butt, and 25- or 32-round magazines are inserted from below the grip, a system that helps the firer replace magazines quickly.

Early models of the Uzi had a fixed wooden stock, although most have since been fitted with a folding metal example (as shown above). The grip is positioned roughly at the point of balance, which makes the weapon much easier to control when firing bursts or from one hand. The Uzi has now been in service for 50 years.

SPECIFICATIONS

Manufacturer:	*Israel Military Industries*
Type:	*submachine gun*
Calibre:	*9mm*
Cartridge:	*9mm Parabellum*
Length:	*470–650mm (18.5–25.6in)*
Length of barrel:	*260mm (10.23in)*
Number of grooves:	*6*
Weight:	*3.75kg (8.25lb)*
Cyclic rate of fire:	*600rpm*
Practical rate of fire:	*200rpm*
Operation:	*blowback*
Magazine capacity:	*25 or 32*
Fire mode:	*semi-, full-auto*
Muzzle velocity:	*400mps (1312fps)*
Maximum range:	*200m (656ft)*
Effective range:	*50m (164ft)*
Entered service:	*1954*

AR-70/90

This weapon was the result of the Italian Army's decision to adopt a small-bore assault rifle for its troops in the 1960s. The Beretta AR-70 family of weapons was selected, including the AR-70 assault rifle, SC-70 carbine and LM-70 light machine gun. The AR-70 copied many features of the AK-47, though with certain modifications. For example, while the AK-47 has long-stroke gas drives with a gas piston permanently attached to the bolt carrier, the AR-70 has a short-stroke gas drive with a separated gas piston. The charging handle is fixed to the bolt carrier, while the gas regulator has two positions for normal or heavy duty modes of operation.

In the late 1980s, the Italian Army decided to adopt the 5.56mm round throughout its units in line with other Western armies, and in the subsequent assault rifle trials the Beretta AR-70/90 rifle was selected. The new weapon had a number of improvements, including a strengthened receiver, a reshaped butt to give a straight-line layout, and a detachable carrying handle. There are a number of variants of this weapon, including the SC-70/90 (a folding butt version of the AR-70/90) and the SCS-70/90 (a short-barrelled variant of the SC-70/90, which has a folding butt but no gas regulator and therefore has no ability to fire rifle grenades).

SPECIFICATIONS

Manufacturer:	Beretta
Type:	assault rifle
Calibre:	5.56mm
Cartridge:	5.56 x 45mm NATO
Length:	998mm (39.29in)
Length of barrel:	450mm (17.71in)
Number of grooves:	6
Weight:	3.99kg (8.77lb)
Cyclic rate of fire:	625rpm
Practical rate of fire:	150rpm
Operation:	gas
Magazine capacity:	30
Fire mode:	semi-, full-auto, three-round burst
Muzzle velocity:	930mps (3050fps)
Maximum range:	1000m (3280ft)
Effective range:	400m (1312ft)
Entered service:	1990 (AR-70/90)

MODEL 12

The Beretta Model 12 submachine gun was developed in 1959 and was adopted by the Italian Army, the *Carabinieri*, and by other military and police agencies around the world. The Model 12 is a recoil-operated, selective-fire gun that operates from an open bolt. The firing pin is fixed to the bolt, which "sleeves" around the rear part of the barrel to reduce the overall length and barrel jumping during full-automatic fire. The receiver, both handles and magazine veil are made from stamped steel. The charging handle is located on the left side. The two pistol grips are located at each end of the body, and the Model 12 has a push-through selector lever just in front of and above the rear grip, behind which is a push-button safety catch. The safety catch actually unlocks the main safety system, which is a lever built into the front of the grip. Unless the grip safety is squeezed, the bolt will not move, whether it is in the cocked or uncocked state.

The Model S version, introduced in 1983, has an automatic safety catch at the front side of the grip, as well as a three-position safety/fire selector and improved butt catch operation. This version also has improved sights and has its external surfaces coated in a protective epoxy resin finish. The Model 12 may be fitted with either a side-folding metallic stock or a fixed stock.

SPECIFICATIONS

Manufacturer:	*Beretta*
Type:	*submachine gun*
Calibre:	*9mm*
Cartridge:	*9mm Parabellum*
Length:	*417–660mm (16.43–26in)*
Length of barrel:	*200mm (7.9in)*
Number of grooves:	*6*
Weight:	*3.4kg (7.48lb)*
Cyclic rate of fire:	*550rpm*
Practical rate of fire:	*200rpm*
Operation:	*blowback*
Magazine capacity:	*20, 32 or 40*
Fire mode:	*semi-, full-auto*
Muzzle velocity:	*380mps (1250fps)*
Maximum range:	*200m (656ft)*
Effective range:	*50m (164ft)*
Entered service:	*1959*

SC-70/90

This weapon is an assault carbine version of the AR-70/90. It is a light rifle ideally suited to security/police work. Essentially a folding-butt version of the AR-70/90, it has a strengthened receiver and a detachable carrying handle. Automatic models of this sort of rifle are perfect for commando missions, where long-range precision and long barrels are not needed. Because of these attributes, it is used by the *Gruppo Intervento Speciale* (GIS) of Italy, a unit which numbers only 50 members.

The SCS-70/90 is the special-purpose version of this rifle. It features the folding stock and a shorter barrel. The SC-70/90 and SCS-70/90 are in service with the COMSUBIN (Italian Navy Commandos).

Both weapons can take M16-type magazines, and are gas operated with a rotating bolt. The SCS-70/90 has no gas regulator and cannot fire rifle grenades, and the SCP-70/90 variant is similar to the SCS-70/90 but with a gas regulator and attachable grenade launcher.

The trigger mechanism of the AR-70/90 range of rifles allows single shots, three-round bursts or full-automatic fire. In addition, all variants have strong receivers and have been designed to facilitate ease of field stripping and maintenance. The bayonet shown in the photograph comes with the weapon as standard.

SPECIFICATIONS

Manufacturer:	Beretta
Type:	assault rifle
Calibre:	5.56mm
Cartridge:	5.56 x 45mm NATO
Length:	757–986mm (29.8–38.8in)
Length of barrel:	450mm (17.8in)
Number of grooves:	6
Weight:	3.99kg (8.77lb)
Cyclic rate of fire:	700rpm
Practical rate of fire:	150rpm
Operation:	gas
Magazine capacity:	30
Fire mode:	semi-, full-auto, three-round burst
Muzzle velocity:	960mps (3150fps)
Maximum range:	1000m (3280ft)
Effective range:	400m (1312ft)
Entered service:	1990

SPECTRE

The Spectre submachine gun was developed by the Italian company SITES in the mid-1980s. It was designed primarily for close-quarters combat, such as counter-terrorist or police operations, where compact size, instant firepower at short ranges and safety of operations are paramount. The Spectre is a recoil-operated, automatic firearm which fires from a closed bolt. The trigger group is more similar to a handgun than to a submachine gun, i.e. double-action (a firing mechanism employing a hammer, in which the hammer can be raised and cocked by the thumb and then released by the trigger; alternatively it can be raised, cocked and released by a longer pull of the trigger) without manual safety. This means that the weapon can be carried with a loaded chamber and hammer down, and then fired immediately simply by pressing the trigger.

The receiver of the Spectre is made from stamped steel and the magazine is of an unusually thick four-column design. The bolt is so designed that it acts as an air pump to push air through the barrel shroud to provide additional cooling for the barrel and action (very useful when firing long bursts). The Spectre has a top-folding stock, pistol grip and polymer forward handle. Its compact size makes it ideal for police and special forces use, especially for undercover and plainclothes operatives.

SPECIFICATIONS

Manufacturer:	*SITES*
Type:	*police submachine gun*
Calibre:	*9mm*
Cartridge:	*9mm Parabellum*
Length:	*350–580mm (13.78–22.83in)*
Length of barrel:	*130mm (5.12in)*
Number of grooves:	*4*
Weight:	*2.9kg (6.38lb)*
Cyclic rate of fire:	*850rpm*
Practical rate of fire:	*200rpm*
Operation:	*blowback*
Magazine capacity:	*30 or 50*
Fire mode:	*semi-, full-auto*
Muzzle velocity:	*400mps (1312fps)*
Maximum range:	*200m (656ft)*
Effective range:	*50m (164ft)*
Entered service:	*1985*

AK-101

In its effort to earn hard currency, Kalashnikov introduced the Hundred series, which is essentially the same as the older designs but in NATO calibres.

The operation is the tried-and tested Kalashnikov method: reloading is based on using the energy of propellant gases, which are driven into the gas cylinder located on top of the barrel. When fired, some of the propellant combustion gases, pushing the bullet along the bore channel, escape into the gas cylinder and exert pressure on the front surface of the piston. The whole group being driven rearwards, the bolt turns to the right and disengages its two locking lugs from their recesses in the receiver. The extractor claw removes the empty case from the chamber, and the ejector disposes of it through the opening in the right side of the top cover. As the bolt carrier travels farther, the single-strand recoil spring is compressed and the hammer is cocked and engaged with the auto-safety cocking cam. The cycle thus completed, the bolt group begins its return travel driven by the recoil spring. The mechanism goes forward, another round is stripped from the magazine and chambered, the bolt turns left to lock the chamber, while the bolt carrier releases the hammer from the auto-safety sear. With the hammer cocked and the bolt locked, the rifle is ready to fire again.

SPECIFICATIONS

Manufacturer:	Kalashnikov
Type:	assault rifle
Calibre:	5.56mm
Cartridge:	5.56 x 45mm NATO
Length:	943mm (37.12in)
Length of barrel:	415mm (16.34in)
Number of grooves:	4
Weight:	3.4kg (7.48lb)
Cyclic rate of fire:	600rpm
Practical rate of fire:	400rpm
Operation:	gas
Magazine capacity:	30
Fire mode:	semi-, full-auto
Muzzle velocity:	910mps (2985fps)
Maximum range:	1000m (3280ft)
Effective range:	400m (1312ft)
Entered service:	1988

AK-47

One of the greatest assault rifles of all time, AK-47 stands for *Avtomat Kalashnikova, Model of 1947*. The AK-47 was designed by legendary weapons designer M.T. Kalashnikov in the mid-1940s, and was adopted by the Soviet Army in 1949. It was manufactured in huge numbers, for both internal use and export. Many countries, such as Romania, Bulgaria, East Germany, China and others also manufactured clones of the AK, and it is still built around the world in its various versions.

The AK-47's fire selector/safety switch is located on the right side of the receiver, and has three positions: "Safe" (upper position), "Auto" (middle) and "Single-shot" (lower position). The safety switch is somewhat uncomfortable to operate, though. The AK features open iron sights, with the front sight adjustable for windage and the rear sight adjustable for elevation and marked in hundreds of metres. The AK's stock and grip are made of wood.

The legendary reliability of the AK comes from its simple design and overpowered gas drive. When operating in normal conditions, for example, the bolt carrier/bolt group moves at high speed and strikes hard against the rear wall of the receiver and against the front wall of the receiver on the way back. This decreases accuracy, but gives the system the power needed to operate with a fouled and dirty receiver.

SPECIFICATIONS

Manufacturer:	*Kalashnikov*
Type:	*assault rifle*
Calibre:	*7.62mm*
Cartridge:	*7.62 x 39mm M1943*
Length:	*869mm (34.21ft)*
Length of barrel:	*414mm (16.3in)*
Number of grooves:	*4*
Weight:	*4.3kg (9.46lb)*
Cyclic rate of fire:	*775rpm*
Practical rate of fire:	*400rpm*
Operation:	*gas*
Magazine capacity:	*30*
Fire mode:	*semi-, full-auto*
Muzzle velocity:	*710mps (2329fps)*
Maximum range:	*1000m (3280ft)*
Effective range:	*400m (1312ft)*
Entered service:	*1949*

AK-74

This weapon, developed for use by motorized infantry, became operational in 1974. Unlike the AKM (which was essentially a modified AK-47), the AK-74 has a number of distinctive features. The foresight bracket, for example, has two protruding cylindrical sleeves. The front one is threaded for the attachment of the recoil compensator, while the rear one has a lug with a hole for the cleaning rod. The elongated recoil compensator comprises two chambers. The first chamber is a cylinder with a hole for the bullet passage, three top holes for escape of the powder gases and two slits on the left and right of the diaphragm. The second chamber has wide openings on the right and left, and a diaphragm at the front with holes for the bullet exit. The diaphragm edges are also bevelled to ensure the directed gases escape. The butt plate is made of rubber, with transverse grooves to improve the steadiness of the weapon against the shoulder.

The main difference between this weapon and the AKM, of course, is the reduced calibre: 5.45mm. The AK-74 comes with a bayonet, and the BG15 grenade launcher can also be attached under the barrel. As with the AK-47, this weapon has been copied in numerous countries, with clones in China and the former Yugoslavia being chambered for the NATO 5.56mm cartridge.

SPECIFICATIONS

Manufacturer:	Kalashnikov
Type:	assault rifle
Calibre:	5.45mm
Cartridge:	5.45 x 39.5mm
Length:	928mm (36.53in)
Length of barrel:	400mm (15.75in)
Number of grooves:	4
Weight:	3.86kg (8.49lb)
Cyclic rate of fire:	650rpm
Practical rate of fire:	100rpm
Operation:	gas
Magazine capacity:	30
Fire mode:	semi-, full-auto
Muzzle velocity:	900mps (2953fps)
Maximum range:	900m (2952ft)
Effective range:	400m (1312ft)
Entered service:	1974

AKS-74

The AKS-74, developed for motorized infantry, became operational in 1974. It is essentially the AK-74 with a folding stock for use and storage inside confined spaces. The pistol grip, foregrip, handguard and magazine are all made from glass-filled polyamide material, which saves weight but does not compromise the weapon's overall robustness. The rifle is also used by airborne troops, though in addition to a folding metallic butt there are a number of differences from the motorized infantry model. The foregrip, handguard and magazine, for example, are made from plastic material.

An unusual feature of this weapon is the fitting of a muzzle brake to the end of the barrel, which blows the muzzle gases against deflector plates then out to the side, thus reducing recoil. This, combined with its weight, makes the AKS-74 easier to control on automatic fire mode than other similar rifles. The rifle has a plastic-covered magazine which holds 30 rounds of 5.45mm ammunition. Instead of the stock folding underneath the body, as on the AKM, it folds to the side. The AKS-74 retains the simplicity and reliability of the earlier Kalashnikov designs. Some models have been seen with image intensifying night sights, and some have been used by *Spetsnaz* special forces mounting sound suppressors and firing special subsonic rounds.

SPECIFICATIONS

Manufacturer:	*Kalashnikov*
Type:	*assault rifle*
Calibre:	*5.45mm*
Cartridge:	*5.45 x 39.5mm*
Length:	*690–928mm (27.16–36.53in)*
Length of barrel:	*400mm (15.75in)*
Number of grooves:	*4*
Weight:	*3.86kg (8.49lb)*
Cyclic rate of fire:	*650rpm*
Practical rate of fire:	*100rpm*
Operation:	*gas*
Magazine capacity:	*30*
Fire mode:	*semi-, full-auto*
Muzzle velocity:	*900mps (2953fps)*
Maximum range:	*900m (2952ft)*
Effective range:	*400m (1312ft)*
Entered service:	*1974*

AKS-74U

The AKS-74U is a reduced-calibre version of the AKM-SU, with a much shorter barrel and a conical flash suppressor instead of a muzzle brake (the AKM-SU was itself a shortened version of the AKM-S and was designed for use by mechanized infantry; it had a folding butt, short fore-end, finned expansion chamber and a muzzle brake). Like the AKS-74, it has a folding metal stock which folds to the side. The rear sight is a flip-type U-notch, while the front sight is a cylindrical post. The gun also has an expansion chamber (the device at the end of the barrel functions to bleed off gases which would otherwise cause a violent recoil) and a flash hider. The receiver cover is hinged at the front so it can be opened but not lifted off.

This weapon was designed for use by vehicle crews, and is short enough to be handled easily when the crew enters and exits vehicles. With a loaded weight of 3.1kg (6.82lb), this weapon is considerably lighter than the AK-74 assault rifle and has a somewhat higher rate of fire. The AKS-74U has a greatly reduced range due to its shortened barrel. However, it still has more power and longer range than conventional submachine guns that fire pistol cartridges. The AKS-74U was first seen with Soviet airborne troops in early 1984. However, it may have entered service four years earlier, though precise details are lacking.

SPECIFICATIONS

Manufacturer:	Kalashnikov
Type:	compact assault rifle
Calibre:	5.45mm
Cartridge:	5.45 x 39.5mm
Length:	422–675mm (16.61–26.57in)
Length of barrel:	206mm (8.11in)
Number of grooves:	4
Weight:	2.7kg (5.94lb)
Cyclic rate of fire:	700rpm
Practical rate of fire:	200rpm
Operation:	gas
Magazine capacity:	30
Fire mode:	semi, full-auto
Muzzle velocity:	735mps (2411fps)
Maximum range:	400m (1312ft)
Effective range:	100m (328ft)
Entered service:	1984

DRAGUNOV

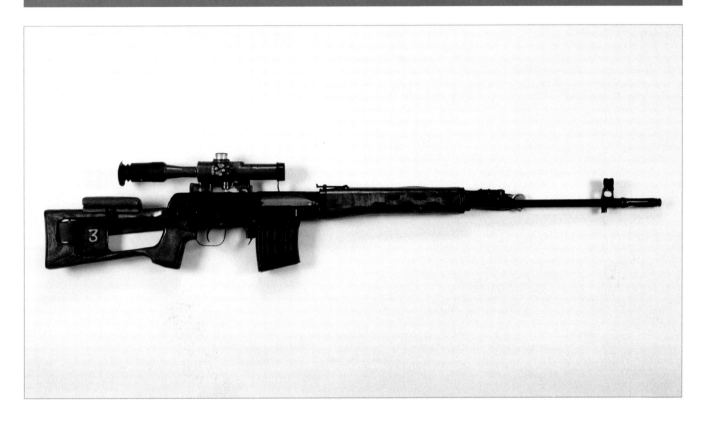

The Dragunov sniper rifle is a gas-operated, semi-automatic weapon which fires the Russian 7.62 x 54Rmm cartridge and uses a detachable 10-round magazine. Its bolt mechanism and gas recovery system are similar to those of the AK and AKM assault rifles, but because of the difference in cartridges it uses parts that are not interchangeable with the assault rifles.

The most distinguishing feature of the SVD is the open buttstock, which has a cheek pad for ease of sighting, and a telescopic sight mounted over the receiver. It also has a combination flash suppressor/compensator. In the field Russian snipers are issued with four magazines, a cleaning kit and an extra battery and lamp for the telescopic sight. The SVD fires approximately 30 rounds per minute in the semi-automatic mode, though rate of fire is dependent upon suitable targets presenting themselves, and has a maximum effective range of 1300m (4265ft) with the four-power telescope, or 800m (2624ft) without the scope. The PSO-1 optical sight has a six-degree field of view and contains an integral, infrared detection aid, and an illuminated rangefinder recticle. Ammunition types used by the Dragunov include light ball, heavy ball, steel core, tracer and anti-tank incendiary. Though now rather long in the tooth, it is still a fine sniper rifle.

SPECIFICATIONS

Manufacturer:	*State Factories*
Type:	*sniper rifle*
Calibre:	*7.62mm*
Cartridge:	*7.62 x 54Rmm*
Length:	*1225mm (48.23in)*
Length of barrel:	*622mm (24.48in)*
Number of grooves:	*4*
Weight:	*4.3kg (9.46lb)*
Cyclic rate of fire:	*n/a*
Practical rate of fire:	*20rpm*
Operation:	*gas*
Magazine capacity:	*10*
Fire mode:	*semi-auto*
Muzzle velocity:	*830mps (2723fps)*
Maximum range:	*3000m (9842ft)*
Effective range:	*1300m (4265ft)*
Entered service:	*1967*

NSV

The NSV is named after its designers – Nikitin, Sokolov and Volkov – and was adopted by the Soviet Army in mid-1970. It is a gas-operated, belt-fed, air-cooled automatic weapon with a horizontal sliding wedge breechblock and a quick-change barrel. It has a long, smooth, unfinned barrel with a conical flash suppressor, and features a rectangular stamped-and-riveted receiver.

A tripod-mounted version of the NSV is available for infantry use in a ground role, but the NSV is more commonly mounted on the turrets of main battle tanks (as shown above), such as the T-64, T-72 and T-80. When mounted on armoured fighting vehicles it is used as an anti-aircraft machine gun. When mounted on vehicles, the NSV can engage both aerial and ground targets. It fires the same 12.7 x 108mm cartridge as the older DShK model 38/46, although the NSV is 11kg (24.2lb) lighter than the earlier weapon.

The NSV has a recoil buffer inside the receiver for smooth operation and all NSVs are issued with the SPP variable magnification scope. The NSV is an extremely reliable and very powerful weapon, capable of piercing 16mm (.63in) of steel armour at a range of 500m (1640ft). It is unsophisticated, but it gets the job done and works in all weather conditions.

SPECIFICATIONS

Manufacturer:	*State Factories*
Type:	*heavy machine gun*
Calibre:	*12.7mm*
Cartridge:	*12.7 x 108mm*
Length:	*1560mm (61.42in)*
Length of barrel:	*1130mm (44.5in)*
Number of grooves:	*8*
Weight:	*25kg (55lb)*
Cyclic rate of fire:	*750rpm*
Practical rate of fire:	*250rpm*
Operation:	*gas*
Magazine capacity:	*50-round link belt*
Fire mode:	*full-auto*
Muzzle velocity:	*845mps (2772fps)*
Maximum range:	*7850m (25,754ft)*
Effective range:	*2000m (6561ft)*
Entered service:	*1970*

PKM

In 1961 the Kalashnikov-designed PK series of machine guns was adopted as the standard general purpose machine gun of the Red Army. Eight years later, in 1969 a product-improved version called the PKM (*Pulemyot Kalashnikova Modernizirovanniy*) was introduced, the main differences between the two models being a smooth barrel and lighter components.

The PKM has a rotating bolt with two locking lugs, similar to the AK bolt, though the PKM's bolt is larger and more robust. Because the PK fires from an open bolt, the firing pin is temporarily fixed on the bolt carrier and can be removed with the bolt. However, while the bolt is rotating along its carrier guideway, the firing pin stays locked on the bolt carrier. It will project and strike a primer while the bolt rotates to engage on the locking lugs. The PKM's bolt carrier is similar to the AK slide, though it is bigger, heavier and has a less complex shape.

The PK family has the gas piston and tube mounted beneath the barrel. The gas tube is fixed on the receiver by a spring steel latch, and it can be separated for cleaning purposes. A simple plastic pistol grip and trigger are underneath the receiver, and a folding bipod is attached to the front of the gas cylinder. As the bipod comes off with the barrel, the gun has to be supported during barrel changes.

SPECIFICATIONS

Manufacturer:	*Kalashnikov*
Type:	*general purpose machine gun*
Calibre:	*7.62mm*
Cartridge:	*7.62 x 54Rmm*
Length:	*1160mm (45.67in)*
Length of barrel:	*658mm (25.9in)*
Number of grooves:	*4*
Weight:	*9kg (19.8lb)*
Cyclic rate of fire:	*700rpm*
Practical rate of fire:	*250rpm*
Operation:	*gas*
Magazine capacity:	*metal belt*
Fire mode:	*full-auto*
Muzzle velocity:	*825mps (2706fps)*
Maximum range:	*3800m (12,467ft)*
Effective range:	*1000m (3280ft)*
Entered service:	*1969*

RPK

The RPK (*Ruchnoi Pulemet Kalashnikova* – Kalashnikov light machine gun) was developed as a light support weapon, and in Soviet service one was issued to each 10-man Red Army infantry squad (it entered service in 1959). The gun replaced the belt-fed RPD in the infantry section. Essentially the RPK is an AK-47 assault rifle with a sturdier receiver, heavier and longer, non-detachable barrel (to increase muzzle velocity), and re-contoured wooden buttstock. The sights were re-calibrated because of the longer barrel, and the rear sight has windage adjustments. The non-detachable, folding bipod (to stabilize the weapon during firing) is mounted under the muzzle. The RPK can be fed from a special 40-round box or a 75-round drum magazine, as well as from standard AK-47-type 30-round box magazines. The paratrooper version of the RPK, called the RPK-S, had a side-folding wooden buttstock.

There is no changeable barrel, which means users have to be careful to avoid overheating and excessive barrel wear. There is a cleaning rod beneath the barrel, with a gas cylinder on top of the barrel. The machine gun, like all Kalashnikov products, is very robust and works in adverse conditions. It is also light and simple to use. A little dated now, it is still in service with Russian reserve and second-line units.

SPECIFICATIONS

Manufacturer:	Kalashnikov
Type:	light machine gun
Calibre:	7.62mm
Cartridge:	7.62 x 39mm M1943
Length:	1041mm (41in)
Length of barrel:	590mm (23.22in)
Number of grooves:	4
Weight:	4.76kg (10.47lb)
Cyclic rate of fire:	600rpm
Practical rate of fire:	200rpm
Operation:	gas
Magazine capacity:	30, 40 or 75
Fire mode:	semi-, full-auto
Muzzle velocity:	734mps (2400fps)
Maximum range:	3000m (9842ft)
Effective range:	1500m (4921ft)
Entered service:	1959

RPK-74

J ust as the RPK is the squad machine-gun version of the AK-47 assault rifle, the RPK-74 is a machine-gun version of the AK-74 assault rifle, firing the same ammunition. The RPKS-74 is a folding-stock version of the weapon. Instead of the prominent muzzle brake used on the AK-74, the machine gun version has a short flash suppressor. As can be seen in the photograph above, the magazine is longer than that normally used on the AK-74, though the different-sized magazines are interchangeable. The RPK-74 has a bipod, though it is high-set to accommodate the longer magazine. It also has a drop-curved machine-gun butt which gives a grip for the non-firing hand.

The 5.45mm round of the RPK-74 has a considerably higher muzzle velocity than the 7.62mm round of the RPK family of weapons. However, both groups probably have the same maximum range – 2500m (8202ft) – and an effective range of 800m (2624ft). Unlike the RPK, the RPK-74 is compatible with the front-firing ports of the BMP infantry vehicle. Since its introduction in the mid-1970s, the RPK-74 has become the standard squad machine gun in Soviet (now Russian) motorized rifle units. It is replacing both the RPK and PKM, which are both 7.62mm weapons. Airborne squads are equipped with the RPKS-74.

SPECIFICATIONS

Manufacturer:	*Kalashnikov*
Type:	*light machine gun*
Calibre:	*5.45mm*
Cartridge:	*5.45 x 39.5mm*
Length:	*1060mm (41.73in)*
Length of barrel:	*616mm (24.25in)*
Number of grooves:	*4*
Weight:	*4.6kg (10.12lb)*
Cyclic rate of fire:	*650rpm*
Practical rate of fire:	*200rpm*
Operation:	*gas*
Magazine capacity:	*30, 40, 45*
Fire mode:	*semi-, full-auto*
Muzzle velocity:	*960mps (3150fps)*
Maximum range:	*2500m (8202ft)*
Effective range:	*800m (2624ft)*
Entered service:	*1974*

CIS 50MG

This heavy machine gun fires from an open bolt and is capable of both semi- and full-automatic fire. The left- or right-hand ammunition feed facility (it feeds a belt in at each side) allows quick changeover of ammunition in the field. In addition, the gun has a quick-change barrel with a fixed headspace, which allows the barrel to be changed within seconds without any adjustment of headspace. As well as the iron sights, the 50MG can accommodate a reflex sight that allows moving or stationary targets to be engaged effectively, and there is a night sight for firing in low-light conditions. The weapon has been designed for easy maintenance without the need for special tools.

The 50MG has a number of mounting options, including a standard M3 tripod, a pintle mount that can be easily adapted for mounting on vehicles and naval craft, and a softmount which enhances controlability and accuracy by reducing recoil.

Tactically, the air-cooled 50MG can be used for a number of roles, including fire support against infantry, vehicle protection, and helicopter armament. The weapon fires standard NATO 12.7mm ammunition, as well as Saboted Light Armour Penetrator (SLAP) rounds, which can penetrate armour plate up to 25mm (.98in) thick up to a range of 1km (.6 miles).

SPECIFICATIONS

Manufacturer:	*Singapore Technologies Kinetics*
Type:	*heavy machine gun*
Calibre:	*12.7mm*
Cartridge:	*.50 Browning*
Length:	*1670mm (66in)*
Length of barrel:	*1141mm (45in)*
Number of grooves:	*6*
Weight:	*30kg (66lb)*
Cyclic rate of fire:	*600rpm*
Practical rate of fire:	*200rpm*
Operation:	*gas*
Magazine capacity:	*disintegrating link belt*
Fire mode:	*semi-, full-auto*
Muzzle velocity:	*890mps (2920fps)*
Maximum range:	*6800m (22,309ft)*
Effective range:	*1830m (6004ft)*
Entered service:	*1988*

SAR 21

The bullpup configuration is now a firm favourite among assault rifle manufacturers, and Singapore Technologies Kinetics has followed the trend by producing the SAR 21 5.56mm model. It features an integrated 1.5 x Optical Scope and Laser Aiming Device for speedy target acquisition. The SAR 21 makes use of high-strength plastics and composites throughout, making it light and extremely rugged. For added protection for the firer, the weapon has a high-pressure vent hole at the chamber and a composite plate at the cheek rest. The whole gun has been ergonomically designed, has excellent balance and combines high accuracy with low recoil.

Maintenance in the field is made easier by the weapon's modular design. The gun breaks down into five sections – barrel group, bolt group, upper receiver group, lower receiver group and magazine – making field stripping and cleaning easy.

The SAR 21 has a number of optional extras, including a laser-aiming device, a visible infrared option, a blank-firing attachment, and bore-sighting equipment. The standard combat sight is located above the optical scope and provides back-up aiming for the soldier. The SAR 21 is a well-designed weapon, though whether it will achieve export sales in a competitive market remains to be seen.

SPECIFICATIONS

Manufacturer:	*Singapore Technologies Kinetics*
Type:	*assault rifle*
Calibre:	*5.56mm*
Cartridge:	*5.56 x 45mm*
Length:	*805mm (31.69in)*
Length of barrel:	*508mm (20in)*
Number of grooves:	*6*
Weight:	*4.28kg (9.41lb)*
Cyclic rate of fire:	*650rpm*
Practical rate of fire:	*150rpm*
Operation:	*gas*
Magazine capacity:	*40*
Fire mode:	*semi-, full-auto*
Muzzle velocity:	*940mps (3084fps)*
Maximum range:	*800m (2624ft)*
Effective range:	*460m (1509ft)*
Entered service:	*unknown*

ULTIMAX

The Ultimax is a very lightweight and mobile light machine gun. It is a gas-operated, rotating-bolt, fully automatic magazine-fed firearm that fires from an open bolt. The gas system has a three-position gas regulator. The overall action design allows the bolt carrier/bolt group to travel all the way back without being stuck into the rear of the receiver, which helps to reduce recoil and improves accuracy. The original Ultimax 100 had a fixed, heavy, air-cooled barrel, but the current Ultimax Mk 3 version has a quick-change detachable barrel available in two lengths: standard – 508mm (20in); and short – 330mm (13in). The buttstock is also detachable and this, combined with its light weight and low recoil, means the Ultimax can be fired from a standing position if necessary, thus making it suitable for close combat and urban operations (though accuracy without the buttstock is reduced). In addition, the pistol grip just forward of the drum magazine facilitates firing from a standing position.

The Ultimax can be fed from 100-round drum magazines or from M16-type box magazines that hold 20 or 30 rounds. The 100-round magazines are ideal for sustained fire, but because of their powerful springs can be reloaded only with the help of magazine-loading tools. As with the SAR 21, the company is hoping for substantial export sales.

SPECIFICATIONS

Manufacturer:	*Singapore Technologies Kinetics*
Type:	*light machine gun*
Calibre:	*5.56mm*
Cartridge:	*5.56 x 45mm NATO*
Length:	*1024mm (40.31in)*
Length of barrel:	*508mm (20in)*
Number of grooves:	*6*
Weight:	*4.9kg (10.78lb)*
Cyclic rate of fire:	*500rpm*
Practical rate of fire:	*200rpm*
Operation:	*gas*
Magazine capacity:	*20, 30 or 100*
Fire mode:	*full-auto*
Muzzle velocity:	*970mps (3182fps)*
Maximum range:	*1500m (4921ft)*
Effective range:	*400m (1312ft)*
Entered service:	*1982*

K2

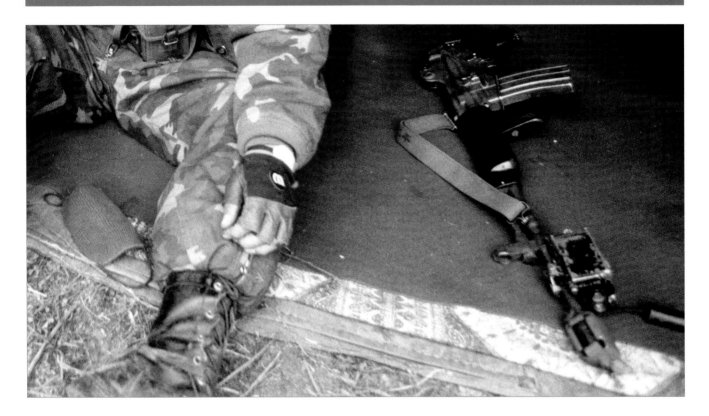

The Daewoo K1 and K2 are the infantry weapons of the South Korean Army, which replaced the US M16A1 assault rifle in South Korean service. The K2 is a select-fire, gas-driven, rotating-bolt firearm which has a bolt/bolt carrier assembly very similar to the one found on the M16. The main difference, though, is that in place of the gas expansion chamber the K2 bolt carrier has a cut slot. In this slot is inserted the rear part of the gas rod, with the gas piston attached to the forward part of the gas rod. In addition, the K2 does not have the recoil buffer that is found on the M16. The receiver is of folding design, and the charging handle is installed on the right side of the bolt carrier. The polymer buttsock folds to the right side of the weapon. The gas system can be tailored for a number of options by means of a four-position switch: rifle grenade firing (the gas port is closed completely); for operations in normal conditions; for operations in adverse conditions; and in conditions of extreme heat.

The K1A1 is a compact version of the K2, which resembles a shortened K2 but uses direct gas impingement on the bolt carrier instead of a gas piston. It has a telescopic stock and shorter barrel. Like the K2 it is also a selective-fire weapon with a three-round burst facility. The specifications at right are for the K2.

SPECIFICATIONS

Manufacturer:	*Daewoo*
Type:	*assault rifle*
Calibre:	*5.56mm*
Cartridge:	*5.56 x 45mm NATO*
Length:	*730–980mm (28.74–38.58in)*
Length of barrel:	*465mm (18.3in)*
Number of grooves:	*6*
Weight:	*3.26kg (7.17lb)*
Cyclic rate of fire:	*800rpm*
Practical rate of fire:	*150rpm*
Operation:	*gas*
Magazine capacity:	*30*
Fire mode:	*semi-, full-auto, three-round burst*
Muzzle velocity:	*920mps (3018fps)*
Maximum range:	*2600m (8530ft)*
Effective range:	*550m (1804ft)*
Entered service:	*1987*

AMELI

The Ameli machine gun was developed by the CETME (now called Empresa Nacional Santa Barbara) company of Spain in 1982, and is in use with the Spanish Army as a standard squad fire-support weapon. Externally similar to the German MG3 machine gun, internally it is much closer to the CETME Model L assault rifle (or Heckler & Koch HK21 machine gun), having a similar, roller, delayed-blowback action.

The Ameli is fired from an open bolt. The barrel is of the quick-change type and it is fed from disposable plastic boxes that can contain either 100 or 200 rounds in belt form. The cyclic rate of fire can be adjusted by means of interchangeable bolts, much like the MG3. With the lighter bolt the rate of fire is about 1200 rounds per minute; with the heavier bolt the rate of fire is about 850–900 rounds per minute. The gun has conventional aperture and post sights, though a night sight can be fitted to the receiver. The Ameli can be vehicle or tripod mounted depending on tactical needs. The weapon is a compact squad automatic weapon which fires NATO 5.56mm ammunition, and has a carrying handle positioned above the rear of the barrel. It has a plastic stock, pistol grip and a flash hider. Despite being a weapon of the 1980s, its lineage can be traced back to the German MG42 of World War II.

SPECIFICATIONS

Manufacturer:	Santa Barbara
Type:	squad automatic weapon
Calibre:	5.56mm
Cartridge:	5.56 x 45mm NATO
Length:	970mm (38.19in)
Length of barrel:	400mm (15.75in)
Number of grooves:	6
Weight:	5.2kg (11.44lb)
Cyclic rate of fire:	1200rpm
Practical rate of fire:	400rpm
Operation:	delayed blowback
Magazine capacity:	100- or 200-round belt
Fire mode:	full-automatic
Muzzle velocity:	875mps (2870fps)
Maximum range:	2000m (6561ft)
Effective range:	800m (2624ft)
Entered service:	1982

CETME

The CETME assault rifle has its origins in the years following World War II, when many German arms designers were, not surprisingly, out of work. Some found employment with Spain's *Centro de Estudios Tecnicos de Materiales Especiales* – CETME (Special Materials Technical Studies Centre). Drawing on their vast wartime experience with the German StG-41 and StG-45 automatic rifles, they designed two prototypes that utilized a blowback/locking roller mechanism. The new weapon was called the Model A and was a reliable and popular weapon.

The latest version of the CETME is a semi-automatic, delayed-blowback gun that utilizes a locking roller to delay the blowback action of the bolt carrier until the pressure in the barrel is reduced to a point where the blowback force is not mechanically harmful. This is a relatively unique feature in military rifles, since most semi-automatics are operated by a separate gas cylinder. The bolt carrier rides a rail on either side of the stainless steel cast receiver, and the forward tube of the bolt carrier sub-assembly rides in its own tube located above the barrel, which also houses the charging handle and a cleaning kit. Like most modern assault rifles, the CETME uses synthetic material for its furniture. There are a number of variants, including the Model LC carbine version and Model LI export model.

SPECIFICATIONS

Manufacturer:	*CETME*
Type:	*assault rifle*
Calibre:	*5.56mm*
Cartridge:	*5.56 x 45mm NATO*
Length:	*925mm (36.42in)*
Length of barrel:	*400mm (15.75in)*
Number of grooves:	*6*
Weight:	*3.4kg (7.48lb)*
Cyclic rate of fire:	*700rpm*
Practical rate of fire:	*200rpm*
Operation:	*delayed blowback*
Magazine capacity:	*12 or 30*
Fire mode:	*semi-, full-auto*
Muzzle velocity:	*875mps (2870fps)*
Maximum range:	*1500m (4921ft)*
Effective range:	*550m (1804ft)*
Entered service:	*1984*

Z-84

The Z-84 submachine gun was developed in the mid-1980s by the Spanish company Star as a compact, lightweight and powerful weapon. Unlike its predecessors, the Z-62 and Z-70/B, the Z-84 is available only in 9mm Luger/Parabellum calibre.

The Z-84 has a stamped steel, two-piece receiver with the magazine housing built into the pistol grip. The bolt is of the wrap-around type, which when in the forward position sleeves around the barrel. The bolt rides on two guide rails and has significant clearance between its sides and the receiver walls, which allows the mechanism to work despite serious fouling. The Z-84 fires from an open bolt (when the bolt is held back from the empty chamber in the cocked condition), and its feed system is designed to accommodate the firing of ammunition used in police operations to achieve better stopping power, such as Soft-Point and Hollow-Point rounds.

The fire-mode selector is located at the left wall of the receiver, and allows for single shots or full-automatic fire depending on the requirement. The two-position flip-up aperture rear sights are graduated for ranges between 100m (328ft) and 200m (656ft). The folding metallic buttstock flips up and forward when not in use. The ejection port is on top of the receiver.

SPECIFICATIONS

Manufacturer:	Star
Type:	submachine gun
Calibre:	9mm
Cartridge:	9mm Parabellum
Length:	410–615mm (16.14–24.21in)
Length of barrel:	215mm (8.46in)
Number of grooves:	6
Weight:	3kg (6.6lb)
Cyclic rate of fire:	650rpm
Practical rate of fire:	200rpm
Operation:	blowback
Magazine capacity:	25 or 30
Fire mode:	semi-, full-auto
Muzzle velocity:	400mps (1312fps)
Maximum range:	150m (492ft)
Effective range:	50m (164ft)
Entered service:	1984

SG550

The SIG SG550 is the official rifle of the Swiss Army, being called the *Sturmgewehr* 90, and replaced the *Sturmgewehr* 57. The SG550 is an improved version of the SG540, which was developed in competition to meet Swish Army requirements in 1984. There is a civilian version of the rifle which is not automatic, and another variant is the SG551, which is slightly shorter than the 550 and is aimed at the police user.

The SG550 was tested under extreme conditions, including winter trials in the Alps. It is designed to reduce the amount of mud, dirt and sand that can get into the working parts, and its gas valve has two settings to ensure reliable cycling under the most extreme conditions (if need be, the user can close the bolt manually).

The SG550 has three modes of fire, including single-shot, three-round burst and full-automatic. In addition, it has special studs and slots in the magazine so that two or three magazines can be clipped together side-by-side. This allows the changing of the magazine by simply pulling the assembly out, shifting it sideways and pushing in the new magazine. The rifle has a folding stock and all features are ambidextrous. The rifle has a night sight on both the front and rear sights, and can mount a scope and light intensifier or infrared sights as well.

SPECIFICATIONS

Manufacturer:	*SIG*
Type:	*assault rifle*
Calibre:	*5.56mm*
Cartridge:	*5.56 x 45mm NATO*
Length:	*772–998mm (30.39–39.29in)*
Length of barrel:	*528mm (20.79in)*
Number of grooves:	*6*
Weight:	*4.1kg (9lb)*
Cyclic rate of fire:	*700rpm*
Practical rate of fire:	*150rpm*
Operation:	*gas*
Magazine capacity:	*20 or 30*
Fire mode:	*semi-, full-auto, three-round burst*
Muzzle velocity:	*980mps (3215fps)*
Maximum range:	*1000m (3280ft)*
Effective range:	*400m (1312ft)*
Entered service:	*1986*

SSG 3000

The Swiss company SIG produce excellent weapons, and this sniper rifle is no exception. The SSG 3000 is based on the equally superb 200STR target rifle, and fulfils a number of requirements: performance, out-of-the-box accuracy, and perfect integration with the shooter. The latter is guaranteed by an ultra-rugged McMillan fibreglass stock that is fully adjustable. The two-stage trigger is also fully adjustable for reach, travel, take-up and weight to fit any shooter's preference.

The SSG 3000 also features a barrel interchange capability (a replacement barrel can be installed in less than two minutes). Other standard features on the SSG 3000 include six massive locking lugs on the bolt, an oversized bolt knob, a tapered, hammer-forged barrel with a flash suppressor, a drop-free five-round magazine, a scope mounting rail machined directly into the steel receiver, and a rail-mounting system on the forearm for bipods or hand stops. The bolt locks directly into the barrel, which has no iron sights but has a muzzle compensator. The barrel and receiver are joined by screw clamps, while the trigger unit and magazine consist of one forged assembly which slots into the receiver. The fore-end is ventilated, and the trigger unit and magazine comprise one forged assembly. All in all this is a first-class sniper rifle.

SPECIFICATIONS

Manufacturer:	SIG
Type:	sniper rifle
Calibre:	7.62mm
Cartridge:	7.62 x 51mm NATO
Length:	1180mm (46.45in)
Length of barrel:	610mm (24in)
Number of grooves:	6
Weight:	5.4kg (11.88lb)
Cyclic rate of fire:	n/a
Practical rate of fire:	5rpm
Operation:	gas
Magazine capacity:	bolt
Fire mode:	single shot
Muzzle velocity:	820mps (2690fps)
Maximum range:	3000m (9842ft)
Effective range:	1000m (3280ft)
Entered service:	1992

SSG550 SNIPER

The SIG SG550 Sniper is a semi-automatic variant of the famous SIG SG550/Stg 90 assault rifle, which seems to be aimed primarily at the civilian market. For example, it is one of the few 5.56mm-calibre sniper rifles around, and for this reason seems suited to police and counter-terrorist units. In essence it is a good short- to medium-range rifle more suited to police or anti-terrorist work than to use in the field. Because it is semi-automatic, a shooter is capable of quick and accurate follow-up shots.

Developed from the SG550 assault rifle, accuracy is improved by the addition of a sensitive double-pull trigger, and also a heavy, extended barrel. A bipod is standard, as is a fully adjustable butt with a cheek rest and a hand stop on the pistol grip. There are no iron sights fitted to this rifle and no muzzle attachments.

The SG550/551SP rifles are commercial versions of the SG550 and 551 respectively, and are intended as sporting weapons or for police and security use. They are restricted to semi-automatic firing and cannot be converted to fire full-automatic. The SIG552 Commando is an ultra-short semi-automatic version of the SG551 SWAT (Special Weapons And Tactics), with a cheek rest and other controls arranged for ambidextrous use. As with all SIG weapons, these rifles are extremely accurate.

SPECIFICATIONS

Manufacturer:	SIG
Type:	sniper rifle
Calibre:	5.56mm
Cartridge:	5.56 x 45mm NATO
Length:	905–1130mm (35.7–44.5)
Length of barrel:	650mm (25.6in)
Number of grooves:	6
Weight:	7.02kg (15.44lb)
Cyclic rate of fire:	n/a
Practical rate of fire:	15rpm
Operation:	gas
Magazine capacity:	20 or 30
Fire mode:	semi-auto
Muzzle velocity:	980mps (3215fps)
Maximum range:	1500m (4921ft)
Effective range:	800m (2624ft)
Entered service:	1985

CAR15

M16 rifles variants, including both the M16A1 and the CAR15, first arrived in Israel during the Yom Kippur War in 1973. Soon after the war the Israel Defence Force (IDF) adopted the Galil assault rifle as its standard-issue weapon, so the M16 did not see much service with the IDF during the 1970s. However, several élite units did test the M16A1, and deployed it in urban counter-terror applications.

Following the success of the M16A1, its smaller brother – the CAR15 – entered service in the late 1970s and was an immediate success. Surprisingly, the first CAR15 configuration to enter IDF service was not the standard version but the CAR15/M203 grenade launcher combination, which was much more comfortable than the few AK47/M203 and Galil/M203 combinations.

The CAR15 model used by the IDF is unique. The first CAR15 models used by the US in the early 1960s – the XM177E1 and XM177E2 – had a 254mm (10in) barrel, which was too short and resulted in sporadic operation. Due to the short barrel, the early CAR15 models also had an excessive muzzle flash, which was a major tactical disadvantage during night-time operations. In order to solve these two issues, the weapons were fitted with a flash suppressor at the tip of the barrel.

SPECIFICATIONS

Manufacturer:	Colt
Type:	carbine
Calibre:	5.56mm
Cartridge:	5.56 x 45mm NATO
Length:	757–838mm (29.8–33in)
Length of barrel:	370mm (14.5in)
Number of grooves:	6
Weight:	2.64kg (5.8lb)
Cyclic rate of fire:	700rpm
Practical rate of fire:	250rpm
Operation:	gas
Magazine capacity:	20 or 30
Fire mode:	semi-, full-auto, three-round burst
Muzzle velocity:	921mps (3022fps)
Maximum range:	1000m (3280ft)
Effective range:	350m (1148ft)
Entered service:	1978

COLT COMMANDO

The Colt Commando was developed as a result of the US experience during the Vietnam War, when it was discovered there was a need for a short carbine similar in size to a submachine gun but which fired rifle ammunition. The Commando is similar to the M16 assault rifle, having the same light alloy construction, rotating bolt action, and utilizing a non-reciprocating charging handle at the rear of the receiver. Because of this, most component parts are interchangeable with the M16. Due to the recoil spring being located inside the butt, the Commando cannot be equipped with a side- or underfolding stock without some redesigning. Current Colt Commando assault carbines are issued with standard M16-type 30-round magazines, but any other M16-compatible magazine can be used, including the 100-round Beta-C dual drums.

The M6 version uses a shorter barrel, plus a shorter stock, making it close in size to most submachine guns, and is ideal for close-quarter combat, yet also has a greater range. The M6 provides the individual soldier operating in close quarters with the capability to engage targets at extended range with accurate, lethal fire.

The Commando has entered service with US special forces, and is also favoured by Israeli élite units. The Israeli version is described on page 82.

SPECIFICATIONS

Manufacturer:	Colt
Type:	carbine
Calibre:	5.56mm
Cartridge:	5.56 x 45mm NATO
Length:	762mm (30in)
Length of barrel:	292mm (11.5in)
Number of grooves:	6
Weight:	2.43kg (5.38lb)
Cyclic rate of fire:	700rpm
Practical rate of fire:	200rpm
Operation:	gas
Magazine capacity:	30
Fire mode:	semi-, full-auto
Muzzle velocity:	921mps (3022fps)
Maximum range:	1000m (3280ft)
Effective range:	350m (1148ft)
Entered service:	1969

M14

The design of the M14 was first conceived during the final years of World War II. US airborne units wanted a weapon with the lightness and select-fire capabilities of the M1 Carbine, but with the killing power of the M1 Rifle. In May 1944, the development of the new rifle began. The requirements were: it had to weigh no more than 4.1kg (9lb), it had to be capable of selective semi- or full-automatic fire, it had to mount a bipod, it should have at least a 20-round magazine, it must have a folding stock to minimize length, it had to have the capability to launch rifle grenades, and it must use the same basic action as the M1.

The M14 entered service in May 1957 and proved to be a very accurate, reliable, durable and hard-hitting weapon. However, it did not fulfil all the design requirements. Because the 7.62mm NATO round is so powerful, most M14 selector levers were replaced with a special selector to allow only semi-automatic fire, thus doing away with the full-automatic capability. Some criticized the M14 for being too heavy and cumbersome, but many troops liked it for the man-stopping capability of the 7.62mm round. In all 1.5 million were built by the time production ended.

The M14 was subsequently rebuilt into a National Match rifle, in which role it still performs today with outstanding accuracy and reliability.

SPECIFICATIONS

Manufacturer:	*Springfield*
Type:	*assault rifle*
Calibre:	*7.62mm*
Cartridge:	*7.62 x 51mm NATO*
Length:	*1121mm (44.14in)*
Length of barrel:	*559mm (22in)*
Number of grooves:	*4*
Weight:	*3.88kg (8.53lb)*
Cyclic rate of fire:	*750rpm*
Practical rate of fire:	*150rpm*
Operation:	*gas*
Magazine capacity:	*20*
Fire mode:	*semi-, full-auto*
Muzzle velocity:	*853mps (2800fps)*
Maximum range:	*1500m (4921ft)*
Effective range:	*550m (1804ft)*
Entered service:	*1957*

M16A2

General dissatisfaction with the M14 and subsequent numerous studies prompted the US Army to call for the development of a lightweight weapon capable of firing a burst of small-calibre bullets with a controlled dispersion pattern. As a result, the Armalite AR-15 was adopted by the Secretary of Defense as the 5.56mm M16 rifle. There were a number of problems encountered during initial fielding, not least due to the weapon being sold as a self-cleaning gun. However, better training, preventive maintenance and several design changes resulted in the weapon that has become the standard-issue rifle of the US Army, with some 3,690,000 having been manufactured to date. The M16 is a good rifle, but requires careful and regular maintenance to keep it in working order.

The M16A2 version, which was re-rifled to suit the NATO-standard 5.56mm bullet, fires a three-round burst in addition to semi-automatic operation and full-automatic mode. The system incorporates an adjustable rear sight which corrects for both wind and elevation, a heavier barrel with 1-in-7 rifling, and a muzzle compensator to prevent muzzle climb during semi-automatic operation. The M16A2 can also fire 40mm grenades when equipped with the M203 grenade launcher, which is attached to the underside of the barrel. The M203 replaced the M79 grenade launcher.

SPECIFICATIONS

Manufacturer:	Colt and Fabrique Nationale
Type:	assault rifle
Calibre:	5.56mm
Cartridge:	5.56 x 45mm NATO
Length:	1000m (39.37in)
Length of barrel:	508mm (20in)
Number of grooves:	6
Weight:	3.4kg (7.48lb)
Cyclic rate of fire:	800rpm
Practical rate of fire:	150rpm
Operation:	gas
Magazine capacity:	30
Fire mode:	semi-, full-auto, three-round burst
Muzzle velocity:	948mps (3110fps)
Maximum range:	1500m (4921ft)
Effective range:	550m (1804ft)
Entered service:	1982

M2

The Browning M2 .5in (12.7mm) is a World War II-era automatic, belt-fed, air-cooled weapon. It has a back plate with spade grips, a leaf-type rear sight, flash suppressor and a spare barrel assembly. By repositioning some of the component parts, ammunition may be fed from either the left or right side. The M2 is capable of single-shot as well as automatic fire.

Today, the M2 can be found mounted on vehicles as an anti-personnel and anti-aircraft weapon. Associated components are the M63 anti-aircraft mount and the M3 tripod mount, both of which provide stable platforms. The M2 .5in flexible version is used as a ground weapon on the M3 tripod mount, or on various US Navy mounts.

Tactically, the M2 provides suppressive fire for offensive and defensive purposes, and can be used effectively against personnel, light armoured vehicles, low, slow-flying aircraft, and small boats. Its 12.7mm round also has good penetrative power against brickwork and masonry. Amazingly, because of its slow rate of fire and its traversing and elevating mechanism, the M2 was also used to a very limited extent as a sniper weapon during the Vietnam War against fixed installations, such as firebases. The M2 is among the greatest machine guns of all time, and will continue to serve well into the twenty-first century.

SPECIFICATIONS

Manufacturer:	Browning
Type:	heavy machine gun
Calibre:	12.7mm
Cartridge:	.50 Browning
Length:	2559mm (65in)
Length of barrel:	1143mm (45in)
Number of grooves:	8
Weight:	38.1kg (83.82lb)
Cyclic rate of fire:	450–575rpm
Practical rate of fire:	300rpm
Operation:	recoil
Magazine capacity:	110-round metal link belt
Fire mode:	single shot, full-auto
Muzzle velocity:	893mps (2930fps)
Maximum range:	6800m (22,309ft)
Effective range:	1830m (6004ft)
Entered service:	1933

M24

Designed for and used by the United States military, the M24 is also very popular with US Special Weapons And Tactics (SWAT) teams across the USA, and with international military and government agencies. Based on Remington's legendary Model 700(tm) and 40X(tm) rifles, famous for their "out of the box" accuracy, the M24 has quickly gained a reputation for precision among the sniper system community.

The M24 is a conventional-looking bolt-action rifle with a six-shot integral magazine. The stock has an adjustable butt plate and is made from synthetic composite materials with metal-mounting components. The bipod is also fully adjustable to increase accuracy.

An essential element in the M-24's accuracy is its heavy, hammer-forged, stainless-steel barrel. The barrel's unique 5-R rifling delivers the combined advantages of reduced bullet deformation and metallic fouling, even-pressure curves, higher bullet velocities and longer barrel accuracy life. Additionally, the M-24's aramid fibre-reinforced, fibreglass stock with an aluminium bedding block provides exceptional strength and dimensional stability in all weather conditions. Combined with its sophisticated sighting options, the M-24 Sniper Weapon System remains the standard against which all sniper systems are compared.

SPECIFICATIONS

Manufacturer:	Remington
Type:	sniper rifle
Calibre:	7.62mm
Cartridge:	7.62 x 51mm NATO
Length:	1092mm (43in)
Length of barrel:	610mm (24in)
Number of grooves:	4
Weight	5.49kg (12.1lb)
Cyclic rate of fire:	n/a
Practical rate of fire:	10rpm
Operation:	bolt
Magazine capacity:	6
Fire mode:	single shot
Muzzle velocity:	777mps (2550fps)
Maximum range:	2000m (6561ft)
Effective range:	800m (2624ft)
Entered service:	1997

M4 CARBINE

The M4 Carbine is essentially the M16A2 but with a collapsible stock. Because of its compact size, it is ideally suited to special operations work, a capability that was further enhanced with the introduction of the M4 Carbine Special Operations Peculiar Modification Accessory Kit. This includes an x4 day scope which allows soldiers to judge range and then fire more accurately beyond 300m (984ft). In addition, the Reflex sight is designed for close-range engagements. Only one sight, as opposed to the normal two sights, needs to be aligned with the target. The shooter can keep both eyes open while using this accessory, allowing more rapid engagements. The visible laser places a red aiming dot on the target, while the infrared pointer/illuminator is used at night and can only be seen with night-vision goggles. The visible light is a high-intensity rail-mounted flashlight and is best used in buildings.

The forward hand grip helps to stabilize the weapon and also helps keep the hand away from the hand guards and barrel, which become hot during use. The sound suppressor is essentially defensive by reducing noise and flash, thus making it more difficult to discern the direction of fire. To accommodate these accessories, a series of rigid grooved rails replaces the normal hand guards. The M4 has seen extensive service with US élite units.

SPECIFICATIONS

Manufacturer:	*Colt*
Type:	*carbine*
Calibre:	*5.56mm*
Cartridge:	*5.56 x 45mm NATO*
Length:	*757–838mm (29.8–33in)*
Length of barrel:	*370mm (14.57in)*
Number of grooves:	*6*
Weight:	*2.64kg (5.8lb)*
Cyclic rate of fire:	*700rpm*
Practical rate of fire:	*150rpm*
Operation:	*gas*
Magazine capacity:	*20 or 30*
Fire mode:	*semi-, full-auto, three-round burst*
Muzzle velocity:	*948mps (3110fps)*
Maximum range:	*1500m (4921ft)*
Effective range:	*550m (1804ft)*
Entered service:	*1982*

M40

In April 1966, the Remington company in the United States offered the US Marine Corps (USMC) its sniper rifle, which was based on the Model 40XB target rifle. Some 800 rifles were initially offered under the designation M40 Sniper Rifle, and Remington eventually built a total of 995 for the Marines.

In the 1970s the initial M40s began to wear out, and so the Marines began to rebuild their inventory into the M40A1 configuration. The M40A1 was built around the same 700BDL actions, but with a polymer stock and a different scope. In 1996, the US Marines started on the design for the replacement of the M40A1, and the result was the M40A3. The latter uses a Remington 700 short action, with a steel floorplate assembly and a new trigger guard. The stock is a new McMillan A4, with adjustable cheek plate and length of pull. As the M40A1s rotate in for service and repair, they are replaced by M40A3 models. The M40 has no iron sights because the telescopic sight is fitted as standard.

All M40A3s are built by USMC armourers at Quantico, Virginia. The M40A3 is extremely accurate, very rugged and is designed from the ground up to be a superb sniper rifle. Combined with the new M118LR ammunition, it creates a system that is ranked with the best in the world.

SPECIFICATIONS

Manufacturer:	Remington
Type:	sniper rifle
Calibre:	7.62mm
Cartridge:	7.62 x 51mm NATO
Length:	1117mm (43.9in)
Length of barrel:	610mm (24in)
Number of grooves:	4
Weight:	6.57kg (14.45lb)
Cyclic rate of fire:	n/a
Practical rate of fire:	10rpm
Operation:	bolt
Magazine capacity:	5
Fire mode:	single shot
Muzzle velocity:	777mps (2550fps)
Maximum range:	2000m (6561ft)
Effective range:	800m (2624ft)
Entered service:	1996

M60

The M60 machine gun has been the US Army's general purpose machine gun since 1960. It fires the standard NATO 7.62mm round, has a removable barrel which can be easily changed to prevent overheating, an integral, folding bipod, and can also be mounted on a folding tripod.

The M60E2 is a modified M60 designed for coaxial tank mounting. The butt and fore-end are removed and an extension tube is fitted to the barrel, and another to the gas cylinder, which vents the operating gases outside the tank.

The M60E3 version manufactured by Saco is a lightweight, air-cooled, portable or tripod-mounted weapon designed for ground operations. It is gas operated with a fixed headspace and timing which permits rapid changing of barrels. The M60E3 also has a receiver-attached bipod which easily deploys for stability. It has ambidextrous safety, universal sling attachments, a carrying handle on the barrel, and a simplified gas system that does not require safety wire to prevent loosening. However, the lightweight barrel cannot sustain a rapid rate of fire of 200 rounds per minute or over without a catastrophic failure of the barrel.

The E4 version is a further improvement on the E3. It features a strengthened bipod, an improved feed system to give better belt lift, an improved flash eliminator, and an optical sight mount integrated into the receiver cover.

SPECIFICATIONS

Manufacturer:	Bridge & Inland
Type:	general purpose machine gun
Calibre:	7.62mm
Cartridge:	7.62 x 51mm NATO
Length:	1105mm (43.5in)
Length of barrel:	560mm (22.04in)
Number of grooves:	4
Weight:	10.51kg (23.21lb)
Cyclic rate of fire:	550rpm
Practical rate of fire:	200rpm
Operation:	gas
Magazine capacity:	metal link belt
Fire mode:	full-auto
Muzzle velocity:	865mps (2838fps)
Maximum range:	3000m (9842ft)
Effective range:	1000m (3280ft)
Entered service:	1960

M82A1

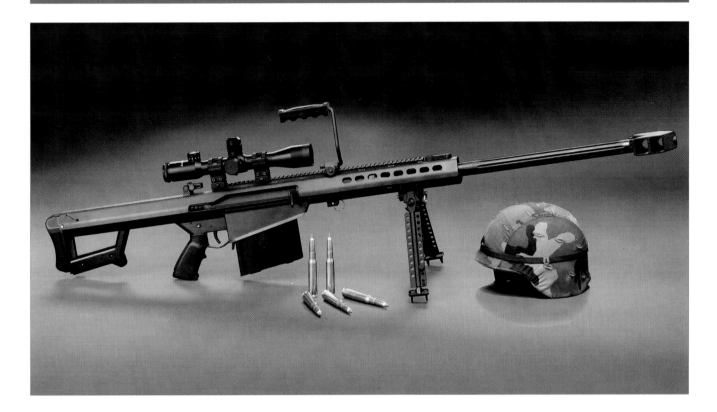

The Barrett M82A1 is an anti-material/sniper rifle, and it is supremely suited for these jobs. The original weapon was designed by Ronald Barrett in the 1980s, and was one of the first semi-automatic rifles chambered for cartridges normally reserved for heavy machine guns. The Barrett was used in the 1991 Gulf War for sniping, and to destroy landmines from a safe distance.

The Barrett is a large rifle, with a total length of 1549mm (61in) and a weight of 13.4kg (29.48lb), which fires the powerful .5in BMG cartridge from a 10-shot magazine. Its layout is conventional, with the magazine in front of the trigger guard, and a mounting for a scope on top of the receiver. The action is of the Short Recoil type, i.e. the recoil of firing the weapon moves the locked barrel/bolt assembly about 53.5mm (2.5in) to the rear, after which the bolt rotates and continues to travel backwards while the barrel stops. The bolt then travels forward again, strips a round out of the magazine and chambers it. Then the bolt rotates again, locking it and the barrel, and the closed assembly moves 53.5mm (2.5in) forward again, thus ending the cycle.

The Barret is truly an awesome weapon, which can disable light-skinned vehicles as well as enemy personnel at greater ranges than other sniper rifles.

SPECIFICATIONS

Manufacturer:	Barrett
Type:	anti-material/sniper rifle
Calibre:	12.7mm
Cartridge:	12.7 x 99mm
Length:	1549mm (61in)
Length of barrel:	737mm (29in)
Number of grooves:	8
Weight:	13.4kg (29.48lb)
Cyclic rate of fire:	n/a
Practical rate of fire:	10rpm
Operation:	recoil
Magazine capacity:	10
Fire mode:	semi-auto
Muzzle velocity:	853mps (2798fps)
Maximum range:	3000m (9842fps)
Effective range:	1500m (4921ft)
Entered service:	1983

M95

The Barrett Model 95 is a relatively small, lightweight 12.7mm-calibre rifle with an emphasis placed on accuracy and durability. The robust bullpup design results in a compact rifle with no sacrifice with regard to accuracy or velocity thanks to its cryogenically treated 737mm (29in) barrel (which is the same length as the Model 82A1). Recoil is reduced by the dual-chamber muzzle brake and specially designed recoil pad.

The rugged three-lug bolt of the Model 95 locks rigidly into the barrel extension to accommodate the widest variety of factory ammunition loads. The adjustable bipod may easily be detached by removing a single quick-release pin. The heavy, smooth barrel has a massive muzzle brake.

The Model 95 is designed to mount a variety of telescopic sights, and with good ammunition this combination results in excellent accuracy. The Model 95 may be disassembled for cleaning without tools, which makes it ideal for field use (Barrett has ongoing research and development contracts with the US Army's Special Forces and US Marine Corps for the development of product improvements to enhance the capability of fielded equipment). The Model 95 is another excellent sniper rifle from Barrett, a company renowned for producing rifles of the highest quality and performance.

SPECIFICATIONS

Manufacturer:	Barrett
Type:	sniper rifle
Calibre:	12.7mm
Cartridge:	12.7 x 99mm
Length:	1143mm (45in)
Length of barrel:	737mm (29in)
Number of grooves:	8
Weight:	10kg (22lb)
Cyclic rate of fire:	n/a
Practical rate of fire:	10rpm
Operation:	bolt
Magazine capacity:	5
Fire mode:	single shot
Muzzle velocity:	853mps (2798fps)
Maximum range:	3000m (9842fps)
Effective range:	1500m (4921ft)
Entered service:	1995

M99

The Barrett Model 99 (Big Shot) Rifle is the latest addition to the Barrett family of 12.7mm-calibre rifles. First shown in 1999, the extremely accurate Big Shot has captured the attention of long-range 12.7mm-calibre shooters around the world. What makes the Big Shot unique is its rugged aluminium alloy receiver, with cantilevered barrel and multi-lug bolt design. The interior of the 838mm (33in) barrel is machined to the same exacting specifications of all Barrett products, and inspected for dimensional compliance with state-of-the-art air gauging. The exterior of the barrel is unfluted to maximize the rigidity and thus the accuracy of the system.

Accurate scope mounting on the Big Shot is facilitated by the M1913 Picatinny (modified Weaver) Rail that is formed as an integral part of the receiver. This rail has become the new industry standard and allows easy removal and re-attachment of scopes with minimal effect on zero. The simple, straightforward design of the Big Shot makes disassembly easy and maintenance very straightforward. Three quick-release pins secure the trigger and bolt guide to the receiver. When these pins are removed the entire rifle can be easily disassembled for cleaning and lubrication. A fourth quick-release pin removes the adjustable bipod to accommodate bench-rest shooting.

SPECIFICATIONS

Manufacturer:	Barrett
Type:	sniper rifle
Calibre:	12.7mm
Cartridge:	12.7 x 99mm
Length:	1280mm (50.39in)
Length of barrel:	838mm (33in)
Number of grooves:	8
Weight:	11.36kg (25lb)
Cyclic rate of fire:	n/a
Practical rate of fire:	10rpm
Operation:	bolt
Magazine capacity:	unknown
Fire mode:	single shot
Muzzle velocity:	unknown
Maximum range:	unknown
Effective range:	unknown
Entered service:	1999

MAC 10

Designed by Gordon Ingram around 1970, this submachine gun was first manufactured by the Military Armament Corporation (MAC), hence its designation, and it was designed to be smaller, more compact and less expensive than other comparative designs. It is one of the most reliable submachine guns in existence. Firing from an open bolt which when closed partially wraps around the barrel, the entire weapon is made from pressed steel plate. It has a phenomenal rate of fire – as high as 1280rpm – and an entire magazine of 32 rounds can be emptied in under 1.5 seconds!

The MAC 10 also became well known for the numerous suppressors that were made for it. These were highly effective, and wrapped with cloth they were excellent for holding on to. The MAC 10 is small enough to be fitted into a briefcase; indeed, several kinds of briefcases were made that not merely allowed the concealed carrying of a silenced MAC 10, but the actual firing of one from inside the briefcase (Heckler & Koch have copied this to allow their MP5K to be fired from a specially designed briefcase). Though the standard magazine for the MAC 10 holds 32 rounds, many different versions can be found.

The MAC 11 is a slightly smaller version, being chambered for the 9mm Short cartridge.

SPECIFICATIONS

Manufacturer:	Military Armament Corporation
Type:	submachine gun
Calibre:	9mm
Cartridge:	9mm Parabellum
Length:	298–559mm (11.73–22in)
Length of barrel:	146mm (5.75in)
Number of grooves:	6
Weight:	2.72kg (5.98lb)
Cyclic rate of fire:	1280rpm
Practical rate of fire:	300rpm
Operation:	blowback
Magazine capacity:	32
Fire mode:	semi-, full-auto
Muzzle velocity:	380mps (1200fps)
Maximum range:	150m (492ft)
Effective range:	50m (164ft)
Entered service:	1971

STONER 63

Though they are no longer in service, the weapons of Eugene Stoner warrant a mention because they laid the foundations for many modern small arms. The Stoner 62 weapon system was based on the 7.62mm NATO cartridge. However, the design was interrupted when it became apparent that the United States was moving over to the 5.56mm round. The new design was then updated to the 63 system, which contained six separate but integrated weapon configurations: carbine, rifle, magazine-fed light machine gun, belt-feed light machine gun, medium machine gun and a fixed machine gun for vehicle mounts.

The Mk 23 (XM-207) was the only one of the designs to see combat, being used by US Navy SEAL teams in the Vietnam War in the 1960s.

Most SEAL Stoners were of the belt-fed, light machine gun variety, such as the Stoner 63A Commando (which had a shortened barrel). The gun used either a 150-round drum that attached beneath the gun and fed from the left, or a 100- or 150-round plastic box that mounted sideways beneath the gun and fed from the left.

In the field Stoners required diligent cleaning, lubrication and inspection of parts. A variation of the Stoner machine gun lives on today with the FN M249 belt- and magazine-fed squad automatic weapon (SAW).

SPECIFICATIONS

Manufacturer:	Cadillac Gage Corporation
Type:	light machine gun
Calibre:	5.56mm
Cartridge:	5.56 x 45mm M193
Length:	1029mm (40.24in)
Length of barrel:	551mm (21.69in)
Number of grooves:	4
Weight:	5.65kg (12.43lb)
Cyclic rate of fire:	700rpm
Practical rate of fire:	200rpm
Operation:	gas
Magazine capacity:	30 or metal link belt
Fire mode:	full-auto
Muzzle velocity:	990mps (3250fps)
Maximum range:	2653m (8704ft)
Effective range:	1000m (3280ft)
Entered service:	1965

INDEX